TRANS LOVE

TRANS LOVE

AN ANTHOLOGY OF TRANSGENDER AND NON-BINARY VOICES

Edited by Freiya Benson

Jessica Kingsley *Publishers*
London and Philadelphia

First published in 2019
by Jessica Kingsley Publishers
73 Collier Street
London N1 9BE, UK
and
400 Market Street, Suite 400
Philadelphia, PA 19106, USA

www.jkp.com

Library of Congress Cataloging in Publication Data
A CIP catalog record for this book is available from the Library of Congress

British Library Cataloguing in Publication Data
A CIP catalogue record for this book is available from the British Library

ISBN 978 1 78592 432 3
eISBN 978 1 78450 804 3

Printed and bound in the United States

Certified Chain of Custody
SUSTAINABLE   Promoting Sustainable Forestry
FORESTRY
INITIATIVE   www.sfiprogram.org
               SFI-01268

SFI label applies to the text stock

CONTENTS

PART 4: FAMILY AND FRIENDSHIP   157

Disclaimer

Self-identity is a hugely personal thing. We all have a lot of words to describe how we identify, and we also all attach various meanings to those words. This book features the work of many different people, and what their identity means to them. The language used in each piece of writing is personal to the individual writing it, and is specific to their experiences and how they see themselves.

ACKNOWLEDGEMENTS

There have been so many people who have been invaluable in putting together this anthology, the list is huge, and I'm eternally grateful to you all.

Thank you to all the people who shared my shout-outs on social media. Thanks also to @AllAboutTrans, @DIVAmagazine, Kat @TopsidePress, Felix and Gregory @OpenBarbers, Sabah, Jo G., Chrissy and Maeve for your support, kindness, sharing and general awesomeness.

Thank you to Sarah and Gwen for letting me share some of the beautiful quotes that get sent to www.genderfork.com, and to all the people who sent in answers to the many questions I asked about love across the internet.

Huge thanks to Lyndsay and Lynn for proofreading, pointing out my shoddy grammar, offering criticism and generally making this book infinitely better.

Thanks to the beautiful people at Allsorts Youth Project, who have listened to me going on and on about this book for a year now, and allowed me the flexibility at work to enable it to happen.

Thank you also to everyone who contributed. I remember at the start of all this thinking that no one will want to write anything for me, and I might as well just give up now. So I'm glad you all proved me wrong with your beautiful, amazing, extraordinary work.

Thank you so much to my mum and dad, for being there, and for being proud of me.

And especially big thanks to Lyndsay, who has been a rock during the whole process of putting this anthology together. Your support and positivity have been a lifeline, and I couldn't have done it without you.

INTRODUCTION

~~~~~~

This is a book about love.

It's about the highs and the lows, the dizzy feeling of euphoria, the dark crashing waves of disappointment, the pain and the joy.

It's also a book about how that works out for trans and non-binary people.

I'm hoping that some of you know what that all means, but equally, maybe you've just picked this up, enticed by the cover, and now you've read that first sentence you're feeling a little confused.

Well first, don't worry! I'm going to run through some definitions, go over the basics and do the groundwork, so that we're all on the same page.

And where better to do that than the first page?

Let's start with the word trans. A trans person is someone who doesn't feel that they are the gender they were given when they were born. For example, when I was born, the doctor looked at my bits and, based on what they saw, decided I was male. This is fair enough – I was after all a tiny baby, and at the time couldn't say,

'Woah there, doc, let's take things a little steadier and see what happens'.

As time went on though, and I started to develop language to describe how I felt, I was able to say, 'Actually, you know what? This doesn't feel right, but I do know how to fix it.'

Obviously, the bit where I fixed it was more than just me going 'I'm a woman', but you get the idea.

The word trans is also a shortened form of the word transgender, which was first (as far as we are aware) used in the 1960s, as an alternative to the word transsexual. It gained more popularity in the 1990s as an umbrella term to describe different gender variant identities, as well as being an identity in its own right.

Today, people largely use trans or transgender depending on personal preference. Both are equally valid and both are words used within and outside the trans community to describe who we are. The word transsexual is also still used by some trans people to describe themselves, but on a less frequent basis. Broadly speaking, it can sometimes be seen as an outdated term to use to describe trans people nowadays, especially in a collective sense, and when used by people from outside the trans community. In relation to this, it is worth mentioning that it's important to respect how trans people describe themselves and to be led by the words they use, be they trans, transgender or transsexual.

For trans people, being who we are is often an easy thing to understand because we all feel this. For people who don't identify as trans though (also known as cis or cisgendered people) it's something that can be a little more challenging to understand.

I've had people ask, 'How do you know you're trans?' And honestly, I just do, in the same way that you may know you're not. It's not the clearest answer, because I don't think there is a clear answer, but like many other things to do with how we feel, like love for instance (see what I did there, eh?), sometimes we just know.

I know that despite being born with a penis, one of the 'traditional' markers of maleness, I am not a man. I know this because I feel it inside, like a wrongness within my core sense of self. I know that I'm not imagining this, because I've spent years exploring this feeling, working out what it means, and along the way I have found lots of other people who feel the same. I also know because, honestly, being trans is pretty hard, and if I didn't feel so strongly about it, like I do, then I'd probably just not do it.

The other word that's going to come up a lot is non-binary. Sometimes it's hyphenated and sometimes it's not. Sometimes it's one word, 'nonbinary' and again, sometimes it's not. For the purposes of this book though, it's all the same thing, and the hyphens, gaps or non-gaps are just a reflection of that particular writer.

Binary, roughly defined, is stuff consisting of, or related to, two things. Examples could include combinations like black and white, one and zero, asleep and awake or, if we're talking gender, male and female.

Non-binary, again roughly defined, is something not related to or consisting of just two things. To put it in another way that's more connected to identity, non-binary is often used in reference to any identity that's not exclusively male or female. This can also include feeling as if you don't fit in at all with either of these binary genders, or if you fluctuate between them, or are outside the gender spectrum, without gender entirely (also known as being agender). Like the word trans, some people view it as an umbrella term, and some people see non-binary as falling under the umbrella of being trans, while others see it as something separate.

(If you want to know more then skip ahead to Meg-John Barker's chapter in this very book!)

As before, when we spoke about the words trans people can use to describe themselves, it's good not to assume, as identity is personal and self-defined, and it's not our place to tell someone how they should be or what words they should use.

Basically, be respectful and be nice.

In this anthology, there is writing by trans people and writing by non-binary people, and hopefully that will also help give you a broader understanding of what these identities mean.

Of course, if you already know all this you're probably good to go, so thank you for waiting while we all catch up a bit.

You're great. (Yes, you!)

What about love?

Ah love. It's a big word to try and define, as it's so widely used in so many different contexts. However, I asked around, and these are some of the many words people used to describe love:

- Intense
- Home
- Everything
- Meaning
- Opening
- Comfort
- Encompassing
- Roots

- Vulnerability
- Connection
- Safety
- Empathy
- Oxytocin
- Seeing
- Scary
- Strong

- Full-on
- Amazing
- Paradox
- Tricky
- Beautiful

- Elusive
- Fleeting
- Missing
- Patient
- Everywhere.

Love is such a big word that the ways to describe it are almost endless. The words we use are powerful and often contradictory because there are so many ways to love, and they're all unique to the individual experiencing it.

People also use the word love when they're really into something, at the end of letters and texts, and as a term of affection when speaking to others (but only in Britain, and possibly only used by British characters in American sitcoms). Amusingly, it's also a score of zero in tennis, which, depending on your experiences of love, could be strangely poignant.

You can use the word love in phrases ('things just didn't work out, I suppose we fell out of love') and as an expression of frustration ('for the love of God', or strangely, 'for the love of Mike', which is a British phrase that hardly anyone uses).

Love is everywhere when it comes to proverbs, and is used worldwide. 'Love is blind' is an obvious one, but others include 'Love itself is calm: turbulence arrives from individuals' (China), 'Love sickness hurts but does not kill' (Mexico), 'In love, beggar and king are equal' (India), 'The heart that loves is always young' (Greece).

The word love, in English, comes from the Middle English word *luf*, which in turn comes from the Old English words *lufu* and *lēof*, which means 'dear'.

Famously, the Greeks had words for the different types of love they experienced. *Agápe* was originally used to mean pure love, often in reference to the love God has for humans, or the love parents have for their children. (In modern Greek *agápi* is also the word used for love.)

Other words include *éros*, which was for passionate hot sex love (and again, in modern Greek, *erotas* roughly translates as intimate love), *philia*, which was for virtuous, loyal, unselfish love, or friendship, and finally *storge*, which was used when talking about families, especially of parents and children, or more abstract love, like that of your country, or favourite activities.

Love has been spoken about, described and defined since we as humans started thinking. It's everywhere, and yet sometimes as elusive and distant as the stars in the sky. Our world revolves around it, and its darker sibling, hate, and there's nothing we can do about it.

We try to do something about it though. Why would we not? It's in our nature. We want to control it and influence its mysterious ways. We research it and talk about it constantly. It's deeply entrenched in our world, our societies, our lives. We've written millions of songs about love and what it does to us, our greatest works of art are about it and we even build apps and algorithms to seek it out. It is intrinsic to our very being.

The next time you see someone, ask them what they want, like really, deep down want, and see what they say. I bet love features strongly.

So love – it's kind of a big deal, right? It's something we all feel, and it's something we are often simultaneously amazing and terrible at. It's as essential to us as the air we breathe, and recent research has shown that feeling unloved and lonely can actually kill us. We need love. It makes life fuller, better and ultimately survivable.

So why write about love and being trans and non-binary?

Well, as a trans woman I think about how love relates to me a lot. That, of course, is not to say that I'm unusual in this. I expect every single person reading this thinks a lot about how love relates to them.

But as a trans woman, I find that love has some extra hurdles and some extra bonuses, and I wanted to write about that. I didn't want it just to be me telling you how it is though. I wanted other voices as well.

So, I started telling people about my idea, and suddenly lots of other people started telling me about how love is for them. A lot of people had a lot to say, and what they were saying was really beautiful and really poignant, and really important.

They spoke about their truths and about how they experience love. And suddenly the book wasn't just about my love, it was about all our loves.

Some of the contributors in this book are out to everyone they know, and some of them are not.

Some are very definitely a particular gender, while others are more fluid, and others still know they don't fit within any traditional gender roles.

Some openly use the terms trans and non-binary, while others will use different words to describe their gender identity, like genderfluid, or genderqueer to give but two. Some of us share this with everyone we meet, intentionally or just because of the way we appear to others, while some of us only share this with a select few we know we can trust.

It's important to say all of this, because just as there's no one way of being in love, there's also no one way of being trans.

Of course, as well as giving people a voice, there's another reason it's important to talk about love and how it relates to us as trans people.

Right now, in the twenty-teens, being trans is a very present thing. Some of it is amazing and celebratory, and there's some remarkable work being done by strong and empowered trans and non-binary people across the globe. Visibility and trans awareness are increasing and things are starting to really change for the better in terms of rights and support.

However, with this societal change and this awareness comes the flip side. Hardly a day goes by without a story somewhere about trans people and the potential threat we present to children, women, families, men, society and the universe.

We are perceived both as some sort of powerful cabal, corrupting and pushing our cis-hating agenda onto the world, and also as predatory weird loners, to be avoided and stared at in the street.

We are told that we are a threat to decent human beings, an abomination, unsightly, a falsehood, something to be feared and ridiculed in equal measure.

Read a newspaper, google stories about trans people, read the comments on articles about us and you'll see this and worse.

Of course, as well as all this we are also fetishised and objectified, because hating us isn't enough.

We're told that passing is the holy grail, by people both inside and outside the community, promoting the feeling that we're deceiving people.

We're grilled by people about what bits we have, what medical procedures we've gone through, how much of a man or woman we really are, if having a penis and breasts turns us on, and oh, could

I screw you just to see what it's like, but not in a gay way obviously. (Yep, someone said that to me. Thanks, internet dating.)

We are invalidated, despite all our best efforts to make ourselves valid.

It's no wonder the trans community has one of the highest suicide rates in the world.

And this is just the start. I haven't mentioned the 'panic defence' that gets used in law courts, where someone's trans status is considered as a potential justification for them being assaulted or murdered, or the countries where you can only transition if you also agree to be sterilised, or the places where we can't even go to the toilet without fear of arrest.

I haven't mentioned all the murders of trans people of colour, and how horrific and brutal they are, or how the perpetrators of these murders are rarely prosecuted.

I haven't even touched on how just walking down the street is sometimes like running the gauntlet, with the stares, insults and threats of violence.

The world for us as trans people is often cruel, and distinctly lacking in love.

Finding something that you connect with, that resonates with you, is a powerful thing, and it can help push back against this tide of hate. It can make us feel less alone, and it also helps us understand and emphathise.

Knowing that there are other people who 'get it' gives us a sense of belonging and can help dilute all that hate.

And I'm not just talking about us as trans people here either.

Differences can be great, they add variety to life, and open us up to new experiences and thoughts, but equally, they're often used as a weapon against us. This feels especially true if you're part of a group of marginalised people, be that because you're trans, a person of colour, or working class, for instance.

Often the media will encourage this agenda of difference equals bad, and sometimes it's easy to believe that, just through the sheer relentlessness of it all.

Take a google of the word transgender and see what the top news story is. Go on, I'll wait.

I've just done it today, and for me the headline is '*Transgender Missouri teen stabbed, had eyes gouged out and her body burned, police say.*' If you're feeling brave you could take a look at the comments, that is if the article allows them.

Pretty awful, right? Pretty much as far from love as you can get.

For trans people this is normal. This level of hate is what we potentially face every time we go outside, every time we meet someone new, every time we come out, every time we interact with the world.

You're probably thinking, though, isn't that a bit over the top? Surely it's not that bad?

And yeah, sometimes it's not. The thing is, though, it's the uncertainty. For instance, every time I meet someone new I have this running commentary in my head. I'm thinking, have they realised I'm trans? If they haven't, when will they? When they do, are they going to be all weird? What does being trans even mean to them?

I don't know how much they know about being trans, I don't know if it's good stuff, or horrible stuff, or nothing at all. I don't know if they think they're talking to a cis woman, and I don't know how they'll react when they realise they're not.

It's complex and overwhelming and, honestly, just super tiring.

Hold on though, this is all pretty full on and kind of hatey, and I thought this book was about love? Well, my curious and outspoken friends, it is. The thing is, however, in order to understand about love, especially in relation to trans people, you need to know what we're up against.

You need to know that other people will murder us because of who we are (and especially if you also happen to be a trans person of colour), you need to know that walking down the street is often an ordeal in itself for us, that people stare, and shout and threaten us, because they see us existing.

You need to know this, because it's important. Imagine if you were constantly told that who you are isn't valid. That you are so different that you are wrong. Imagine what that does to you and how that would make you feel. Imagine that overwhelming sense of fear and rejection.

Imagine how alone that would make you feel.

It makes love seems like a distant dream. It goes without saying that the knock-on effects of this can be huge.

Some of us feel we'll never find someone to love us again, or even at all, while others lose the love of families, friends and partners. The feeling of loss, of losing something you previously loved, needed or took for granted, is a strong one and it's something we can all relate to.

And when it's connected to something fundamental to yourself, rooted to the core of who you are? Well that pain, it cuts deep.

So, love. Love is something we need more of. Love is something we need to talk about more, love is something that can help with all this pain, this loss, this hate.

Yes, sometimes loving is hard, but hate is killing us. It's not just the individual hate we all feel, it's the collective hate. It oppresses us, it crushes the life out of us, it blinds us to the bigger picture. The bigger picture being that we're all in this together. All 7.6 billion of us.

And that isn't a bad thing.

I also think that we all have a collective shared experience that often gets overlooked because of this focus on what divides us. For instance, we all experience love, however we identify, and it's important to remember that, because with that shared experience comes something remarkable.

Think about something meaningful that's happened to you. Then think about the feelings you get knowing that someone else has shared that experience, those feelings.

For example, when someone is sharing something with you and you think YES! I know that thing! Isn't it a wonderful feeling? Doesn't it make you feel connected, less alone, more human?

The funny thing is as well that often it doesn't matter if the thing being shared is good or bad. You still feel connected, despite any perceived differences you previously had.

A while ago I read a book by Katie Green called *Lighter Than My Shadow*. It's about the author's struggles with eating disorders, and in places it's understandably pretty heavy. This book moved me so much, mainly because I related to a lot of what Katie wrote. We've never met, or even corresponded, and as far as I know we have nothing in common other than our feelings around food, but that shared experience still felt powerful despite all this.

Hearing about someone's experience and getting it is important to us as a society and individuals. It gives us understanding, empathy and, ultimately, love, both for ourselves and for each other.

As we're seeing more and more, 'Me too' can be a world-changing sentiment.

What I want this book to be

So, as I mentioned back at the start, I want to make a book about love, and being trans.

I want this anthology to be a positive and empowering collection of writing. I want the work in it to challenge the narrative that all trans and non-binary people are suffering, and that we are unable to experience love.

That's not to say it won't feature negative stuff, because that is a part of life, it's just there's also so much more, and I feel really strongly that we all need to hear about that as well.

For some of the people in this book, it'll be the first time something of theirs is published, while for others this may be a regular thing that happens. Most of the writers in this anthology identify as trans/non-binary but there a couple of pieces by cisgender people as well, which I've included because of their unique and important connections to the trans people in their lives. The important thing is that I've tried to get a wide range of voices, writing about a variety of different types of love because I want to make something that speaks about actual people's experiences, through whatever medium works best for them.

Because of this you'll find poetry and prose in this collection. I've tried to categorise different themes together, but as we all know, despite our best efforts, love refuses to be categorised, and so there's a lot of crossover. You'll find chapters about what it means to be non-binary and in love alongside one-line quotes about the last time someone said 'I love you'. You'll find messages trans people get sent on dating apps, epic poems about Medusa, ghost stories from Japan, and essays on selfies and self-love. In between these chapters, you'll also find quotes from people who answered some questions about love I posed on the internet.

Some of the writing will be more creative, and some more academic, but all of it will be real and authentic. All of it will be from the heart, and all of it will be written in a way that enables that writer to say what they want to say.

I hope that you'll find something that resonates with you among all these amazing pieces of work, because that's something unbelievably important right now. I hope that some of it makes you think, and that you come away from this book with a better understanding of how love is for trans and non-binary people, because although maybe my experience of love is different from yours, underneath it all there's a common ground.

Love is a complex thing, it's never easy and it's ever present. We fall into it and out of it, and eventually it gets us all.

These are the stories of how it does that.

These are the stories of our lives.

♡

ON LOVE – LOVE IN A SENTENCE

~~~~~~~~~

How would you describe love, using just one sentence?

If the heart is a warp core, then love is like antimatter to fuel it.

There is no 'true love'; love is how you feel and not how you think it is.

Trans love is seeing a person as they are, being as free from prejudice as possible.

Loving yourself enough to allow yourself to express your gender however feels right.

Love leads us out of the dark and towards one another.

Love has the power to stop and start hearts like no other feeling.

Someone who sees me for everything I am before they see me as trans.

Love is kindness, wonder, beauty, lifesaving, gut wrenching, painful – a part of life's experience I would not give up.

It's better to have no love at all than to mistake bad love for good.

Love is wanting someone to be happy, love is selfless, love is kind.

Every emotion in one.

Love is the only thing that has hurt me and healed me in equal measure.

Pain, the good and bad sorts.

Painful but completely worth it.

Love is a decision; each and every day.

Love is a way of being in and of and open to the world, through and with and for other beings, including your many selves.

Feeling excited to just be alive at the same time as the other person or people.

Love is wanting the best for each other.

When I tell you I love you it means I am there for you and will do whatever I can to make your life easier.

Compassion that bites.

Being transgender means love is tainted with poison.

Love is the best worst feeling in the world.

Love will save us all, even if we don't want it to.

Having love constantly amazes and surprises me.

Love is powerful, unruly, intense, beautiful and constantly unexpected.

Love is appreciation beyond words.

PART 1
SEX AND RELATIONSHIPS

Okay, so I'm going to start with something basic and fundamental to this book, and something we all need to hear. This is also something we, as trans people, especially need to hear. Ready?

Love is a fundamental human right, you deserve to have it and you can have it.

You are not less deserving of love because you are trans.

To which you may reply, 'Yeah, but can I have love?' 'How do you know?' 'You don't know me; you don't know that's true.'

All of these things are valid points, and some of them may well feel very present and ringing with truth, but again, love is a fundamental human right, you deserve to have it, and you can have it. You are not less deserving of love because you are trans.

I know that repeating something doesn't make it true, right? If it did, then I'd be repeating *a lot* of things. I'm not even joking, I have a list just in case science makes this a reality someday.

But still, let's break it down.

Love, as we all know, is a bit like birthdays. What? I hear you cry. Do you mean that love only happens once a year, and the build up to it is great, but as you get older it just becomes more and more of an anti-climax?

Well, no (although also, maybe yes, a bit).

What I mean is that love is something we all experience, like birthdays, and that sometimes, like birthday presents, we receive, and sometimes we give.

Either way, it's pretty good, and we feel pretty good. We all know love. We all give out love, and if we're lucky, and the stars align, sometimes we receive it.

Everyone, at some point in their lives, has or will experience love. I'm not just talking about everyone's favourite type of love (the getting it on with the person/people of your dreams) either.

There's family and friends, there's your cat, or dog, there's that moment where you think to yourself, hell yeah, I'm pretty fine today (the love we all need and the love that's hardest to find).

We all know love. We all will experience love. It doesn't have to be a grand, earth-shattering thing either; for instance, I love that musical episode of *Buffy the Vampire Slayer*. It makes me feel happy when I'm sad, it soothes and distracts me from the rest of the world, and I love it. Yes, it's an episode of a television programme about a girl fighting monsters, not a real-life person, but it evokes the same emotions I feel when I do experience love from another person.

Obviously, the feeling I get from the love I experience with another person or people has the potential to grow into something more earth shattering, whereas the love I feel for *Buffy* is more of the moment, and maybe less about the shattering of earths, but on a very basic level we are talking about the same thing. It's a strong feeling that makes you feel warm, and ultimately better, even if just for a while.

So, love. We've all experienced it, in some shape or form, even us as trans and non-binary people. Except well, that's it, isn't it?

We've all experienced love as people, but once you bring being trans into it sometimes things change. Here's a really simple example.

I've used Tinder for dating. Tinder, for those of you still living in 1989 (which to be fair is fine, the music was pretty great) is a dating app where photos come up of people in your area looking for love, and you get to choose whether you like them or not by swiping left or right. If you both like each other then you get the chance to awkwardly text chat and see where it goes.

So anyhow, Tinder, I've used it. As part of the process, you get to make a profile for others to see, so they can decide if they like you or not (which incidentally, when put like that sounds kind of brutal, I know).

You get to choose photos of yourself (best done with a friend or two) and then you write a little bit about yourself. See where this is going?

Do I put I'm trans, or do I not?

It's not obvious from my photos, but some might say it's more apparent when you see me in real life. But equally, why should I have to put that out there? Cis people don't have to put that they are cis, so why should I?

But also, what if I don't and I match with someone and it's going well and we meet and then they realise and are all 'nope'. That's definitely going to suck.

It's a dilemma for sure, so I decided to do both. You know, just to see.

Boy, did I see.

First off, I decided not to put that I'm trans in my profile. I'm bisexual, so I set my filters to see everyone and then I started swiping. (I say 'I' here, but in reality this was more of a team effort – again, get your friends involved!)

The matches started to roll in. Interestingly, I matched with pretty much every man on Tinder in my area. Now I'm not saying that men just swipe to the right (Top Tinder Tip 1: this means you like someone!) for every woman they see on Tinder, but clearly men just swipe to the right *every single time*. Way to make a girl feel special, guys.

I also matched with women as well, but not as much, and with less of an obvious pattern (if you can call swiping right all the time a pattern – I'm looking at you, men of Tinder).

Anyhow, after filtering out the people I knew, like my work colleagues, people I had dated, people my friends had dated and warned me about, the usual really, I started messaging. (Top Tinder Tip 2: try not to feel disheartened if this narrows it down to about three people. Just broaden the area of your search till you don't recognise anyone!)

Again interestingly, it seems men are much more likely to message first. I got some right keen beans within minutes of matching.

'Hey baby, what's yr number?'

'You are hot, I want to fuck you bad.'

'Add me on WhatsApp so we can chat properly.'

'Dick pic?'

Actual dick pic.

So that was nice, but honestly, I wanted to connect a bit more first, because I'd got something to say about who I am. There was plenty of time for dick pics later. (There is not, just to be clear. The only time there is time for dick pics is when they've clearly and consensually been asked for. That is the time for dick pics, not 30 seconds after you've met someone.)

I'm sure you're all wondering right, so how did it go, girl? How do people react when you tell them?

Well.

Example 1: The Blind Panic response

Me: *'So, don't know if you realised from my pics or not but I'm trans :)'*
SILENCE.
Me: *'Ummmm, hello?'*
Tinder: *StallionMan has unmatched you.*

(Top Tinder Tip 3:Unmatching is Tinder's blocking feature in that you both disappear from each other's feeds – it's like getting digitally ghosted.)

Example 2: The Brutally Direct response

Me: *'Hey, as we're sharing stuff about ourselves, just so you know, I'm trans!'*
Them: *'I don't do trans, sorry.'*

Example 3: The Awkward Misdirection response

Me: *'I'm trans!'*

Them: 'Haha, umm, well, I'm not actually looking for anything right now. Don't even know why I'm on this site, lol, ha ummm.'

Example 4: The Gentle Let-Down response

Me: you get the picture, I tell them I'm trans...
Them: 'We can meet, but you'd have to understand it would only be as friends.'

Example 5: The I've-got-no-idea-what-this-means-so-I'm-going-to-say-the-first-thing-that-comes-into-my-head response

Me: 'I am a trans.'
Them: 'OMG. You're a ladyboy?!?!!'

Pretty bleak, eh? (Also, StallionMan wasn't his actual name, just in case the actual StallionMan is reading this and thinking, 'Whhaatttt? But I'd never do that, StallionMan is here for all the ladies'.)

I feel though that maybe I'm being a little harsh. Despite everyone else being harsh to me. Maybe they were all just taken aback – no one likes a surprise, right?

We all want to know where we stand, what's going on, and who someone is, right? Maybe I was just doing this the wrong way.

So I did a new profile, with different, equally hot, pics, and a bio that clearly, right at the top, says I'm trans.

And the tumbleweeds rolled on in.

Okay, so I'm being a little dramatic there for effect. But I did get fewer matches. A lot fewer. I'd give you some numbers, but I didn't actually record any. I know, I know, it's shoddy. I'll hand my quality journalism badge in immediately.

Some of the matches I got were legit, so there is that, and there is hope, but realistically speaking, being trans does affect how you experience love, right from the get go.

If people don't know, and you tell them, it often ends badly. And if people do know, it often doesn't start at all.

The overarching theme I discovered in relation to dating was that once people find out about my identity, they struggle. How this presents itself can range from outright blocking of dating profiles to awkward get-out clauses and long silences. The end result, though, is the same.

To them, I am no longer the person they thought I was. To them, I've deceived and tricked my way into making them find me attractive. If they'd only known, then they'd never have messaged, or swiped right. I am to blame, and really what do I expect anyhow?

When, after I let someone know, they message me back with, 'Wow, I'd never have realised, you're really good' it sometimes feels that what they're actually saying is, 'If you were more obviously trans then I'd never have messaged in the first place.'

The internet allows us to express ourselves more freely than we've ever been able to before. Online dating sites and phone apps allow us to connect with people anywhere, and at any time we like. We have this freedom, often without any meaningful consequence, and so we swipe, and like, and message, and heart.

We rush headlong into this new world, where we can make instant decisions about people based on a photo. It's a world where we don't have to listen to or acknowledge our feelings when we like someone who's different, because they'll always be someone else, someone less different, with the next swipe.

It's a harsher, more brutal world, where rejection is just a swipe away. It's a world where that rejection isn't even something you'd necessarily be aware of, unless of course that rejection is so direct, and so frequent that it's impossible to miss.

As a trans woman, I'm pretty familiar with that.

And, of course, on top of all this there's the fact that we are complex and intricate creatures. Our urge to belong and to be loved can be quite overpowering, and this can add a whole other layer of complexity to navigate.

Something I've done in the past when I get into relationships (and I'm going to hazard a guess here and say that I don't think I'm alone in this) is to really throw myself into them.

By throwing myself into the relationship of course I mean be all intense and full on, with a side of emotional unloading, and eager obsessiveness.

My thinking behind this is a messy combination of contradictions. I feel that if I get involved hard at the start it will make it harder for me to disentangle myself when my self-loathing about deserving love gets too much, but also *I really need you to love me so here is my soul*, and also please never leave me.

I'm sure you'll all agree these reasons totally reinforce how much this is the best plan ever.

So, I've done this quite a bit. I also like to add this classic into the mix from time to time – this is my last chance at a relationship so I must throw myself into it at all costs. And that golden oldie – you're looking as if I'm being too intense so I'm going to play it cool and then be even more intense every time I do see you, to make up for all the times I've not seen you.

Yeah, I'm a real keeper, I know.

For me, a lot of this is to do with being trans. It's also because finding someone who loves you, and you can love back, is hard. It's because I don't want to be alone for the rest of my life, oh, and also because society constantly tells us that we are more valid in a relationship than as a single person, especially as we get older. Just saying.

It's because love is really, really complicated.

With all this in mind then, how can you say we can have love? How can we possibly navigate all this mess, let alone navigate it as a trans person?

You say we've all experienced being loved, but it regularly doesn't feel that way. You say we are deserving of love, and that being trans doesn't mean we are less worthy of this, but really?

How much of this is based in reality? How much of this is just me clinging desperately to a slowly deflating life raft jettisoned from the ship of love, quietly whispering to myself, 'Everything is fine, it's all fine'?

Well, here's the thing. Love is quite time consuming. It rarely happens first time, despite what the movies tell us. Love is also complex, and tricky, especially when it comes to loving other people and them loving you in return. It can be incredibly risky as well, especially if you're trans. It's fraught with rejection, pain and weird feelings that contradict and confuse us.

And, of course, on top of all this, love doesn't just come to you, you do have to put love out there, even if it's just a bit. And that, my beautiful friends, is really, really hard.

It's hard because we're under attack a lot of the time, and those attacks seem especially strong when it comes to dating, and by association, love. It's hard because it feels isolating, and so intrinsically connected to who we are as trans people. It feeds into the cycles of self-loathing and poor self-esteem we develop as we navigate life. Every rejection, every dismissal, every time. It makes putting love out there seem like the last thing we'd want to do.

But if we don't try, if we don't put a little love out there, especially towards ourselves, then love will never truly be ours.

It's not always easy to find love, in fact let's be honest here, it's rarely easy to find love. As trans people, we have a lot of roadblocks and hurdles to navigate, and that can be really soul destroying. The thing is though, we're not alone.

Every single person I know, cis or trans, has experienced how hard it is sometimes to find love. Every single person I know.

We all have stuff that makes things harder, we all have baggage, we are all complicated. True love is not as it is in the movies. It's messy, complex and tricky.

Also, though, it's something attainable. I know this because I both have had it in the past, and I have it now. For a long time, I thought I couldn't have it. I knew love was a fundamental human right, but I didn't think I could have it and, honestly, I didn't think I deserved it.

It was only once I started to explore this, and learn more about who I was, and how I worked, that I started to see things differently.

It isn't easy. You have to be brave, and you will get hurt. Sometimes that hurt is painful beyond belief, so you need to find a way to make it better. I used ice cream, friends and old films. Clichéd I know, but why change a tried and tested method?

The important thing is that you need a way to make the hurt better, because then you can carry on trying to find love, knowing you've got a plan for when it doesn't quite work out.

And the more you explore who you are and what you want, the more you know yourself and how you work, the easier it all becomes. Love is a fundamental human right, you deserve to have it, and you can have it. Being trans should never have to be a limiter on that.

Over the course of the following pages, you'll find work by people who are in love, who are out of love and who are exploring what all this means.

These are their stories about how we learned to love each other. These are the stories of our lives.

GINGERBREAD PEOPLE (A LOVE LETTER)

Jo Green

I looked over at you this morning, sitting there, drawing a pentagram in icing on the gingerbread person, and thought about how remarkable all of this is. Where we started, how far we've come. People always use the saying 'what we've been through', as if moments in life are things that we go through and come out of the other side like wading through mud. You come out the other side different with the remnants of the experience still attached to you. You have new words to describe yourself, like dirty or muddy. I can see how it fits. But I prefer to think of it as running through sprinklers, the warm sun beating down on you, water droplets making thousands of tiny rainbows and stinging your skin. I like to think we come out the other side different but happier for it. That's what I think anyway. We've been through a lot. We've moved countries, changed careers, moved to a new house countless times, we've had different cars (and a few motorcycles for good measure), different pets, changed our tastes in music, changed the movies we like, bought different washing machines, had countless different kettles. That's what I think makes us remarkable, not the kettles specifically, but the sheer volume of changes we've been through.

Sixteen years ago we met, and from the first moment I saw you, I knew I had to have you. Not even in a love-at-first-sight way, more like a weird irrational way that I kept trying to talk myself out of. I couldn't help but feel as if I'd known you forever; I'd find myself holding back from casually touching your shoulder as I walked past. I had a sense of familiarity that had no relation to how well we actually knew each other. I'd just got back into the idea of a relationship and I'd decided I wanted someone different from the boys I'd been with before. I wanted someone who would love me, but most of all I wanted someone I could respect. In my weird way, I had sort of assumed it would be someone my mother would approve of, like a doctor or a lawyer (we both know that her judgement of people is more about what they have attained than who they actually are).

Little did I know, you were exactly what I was looking for. You had this sense about you, like an unwavering belief in yourself. No, not a belief. Belief implies trust in something that you can't see. You had an unwavering knowledge of yourself. You knew your power and you completely stood in it. How could I possibly resist? Especially considering how uncertain of myself I was (and still am). I remember that night, that first night. You told me you were trans and that you didn't deserve love, you weren't going to put someone else through that, which confusingly for you made you even more attractive to me. There was no way that someone as strong and powerful as you was going to believe that they weren't worthy of love. We had the perfect balance, I could teach you faith in what you couldn't see and you could teach me how to read the evidence of my achievement. It's strange how 16 years on, we're still learning some of those lessons.

I've been with you for my entire adult life. I can't possibly imagine what life would be like without you. You're the one person who knows me far better than I know myself. When I finally admitted to myself that I am non-binary, you were so unsurprised. It was such a massive revelation for me, it took me years to properly process what that meant, but you just knew. You'd always known, it seems. I'm almost embarrassed to think about how long it took me to finally admit it, but it makes sense that you'd known. Viewed through a trans lens, it makes sense though. I can remember driving around trying to find a realistic looking beard or moustache, I remember buying a wardrobe of men's clothes, trying to find a dress shirt that fitted both my chest and my neck, trying to find a pair of men's trousers that fitted both my hips and my waist, searching for men's shoes in a size five. It's ridiculous that I was doing that ten years before I would finally admit to myself that my gender wasn't what I'd assumed it was. Weird to think that I still have moments where I'm not certain that I'm actually trans.

You taught me that the most incredible thing about trans people is the faith that they have in themselves. You taught me that despite what everyone else tells me, only I know who I am. Your steadfastness in your gender was what taught me that who I am on the inside is so much more important than who people assume I am. And for that I am eternally grateful.

Today when I noticed you noticing the gingerbread people

behind the counter at the coffee shop, I knew you'd want one. When the server asked if I wanted the small tube of icing that is ordinarily reserved for children to decorate their gingerbread biscuits with, I knew this was about to be a silly and fun experience. When all of our discussions referred to gingerbread people instead of the binary gingerbread men, I knew you'd be the person that I'd want to be with for the rest of my life.

LITERACY

. . . .

Grace E. Reynolds

I want you
to read me
like a book.
Skim me first.
Flip through my pages.
And when you have decided,
pore over me at night
under a yellow lamp
when you are home
and warm
and safe
in your bed.
Slide your fingers
over every word.
Look up the ones
you don't know.
Roll them over your tongue
until they are part of you.
Dog-ear my pages.

Break my spine
so I open
to the good parts.
Then lay me on your bedside table
when you are weary,
and in the morning,
pick me up
where you left off.

FIRST DATES AND SEXUAL PRECONCEPTIONS

Freiya Benson

I went on a first date yesterday, and nothing happened. No, wait, that's wrong, I went on a first date yesterday, and what normally happens, didn't.

Let me elaborate.

I sleep with people on first dates. I've done it more times than I'd like to admit, and even though there is nothing inherently wrong with this, I still feel shame, and judgement about saying what I'm saying.

Let me elaborate more.

As a woman, I know how society views us when we say we sleep with people early on in the relationship. As a trans woman, I know that view becomes worse, as it plays into the stereotype of trans women being predatory, promiscuous and easy. I know this because I am a trans woman and have, at various stages in my life, been called all these things.

Of course, these stereotypes are not limited to trans women, but rather all women who sleep with people on first dates. However, the level of judgement and, by association, the level of disgust from other people seems to become almost irrational in its strength of feeling when you put the word trans in front of the word woman.

These stereotypes, these preconceptions, seep into our world and become the first thoughts we have when we talk about these things. I have these thoughts, and that's where the shame and feeling of judgement comes from.

It gets more complicated as well.

As a trans woman, a large part of why I sleep with people early on is because I need to feel wanted, I need to feel attractive and I need to feel normal, because for me, most of the time those things are off limits, especially when it comes to dating.

I've lost count of the number of times I've told someone I'm trans, only for them to turn round and say, 'I don't do trans'.

I've lost count of the number of times people have said how striking I am, only to then immediately block me when I let them know about who I am.

Normal isn't something that comes easily when the rest of the world is telling you that you're anything but.

On the rare times people are alright then I sleep with them. I really go for it, jumping right in at the deep end, not caring that I can't actually swim yet. I think it'll be okay, that maybe this time, if I start to go under the other person will help me, will save me.

Of course, it doesn't work like that. I think that's a given really, as what really happens is I sleep with someone and they get scared off by my frantic intensity as I struggle to grab hold of them.

Or I sleep with someone and they don't even try to be near enough to save me. They say I was an experiment, or that I'm not feminine enough, or that now they think about it maybe they 'don't do trans'.

I know what I have to do. I know that the real problem here is as much to do with me as them. I know that I can blame society, and that society is to blame. I also know, though, that society isn't going to change overnight, or even in my lifetime.

I do know that I can change. I know that, in actuality, if I learn to swim, then maybe I could dive into whichever end of the pool I like and it would be fine.

I know that if I learn to want myself, to see myself as beautiful, to accept that normal is relative, and from within, then maybe I could sleep with people whenever it feels right to.

I went on a first date yesterday, and nothing happened. I think, for the first time, that I'm alright with that.

FREYA

. . . .

Aglaya Khachaturian

Casey, I've been living one of your short stories.
I met this girl, Freya.
Tall, just like me.
On our first meeting, we compared our carefully created vaginas.
We've been cut open by the same hand for fuck sake.

We became friends very quickly.
Shared trauma, hey?
I couldn't make a move tho.
On the one hand I was too vulnerable.
Still healing from the havoc wreaked on my heart.
And my vag wasn't healed either yet.
Then also, I didn't want to be that girl who snatches the newcomer.
I wanted her to figure out what she wanted herself.

In absence of either of us making moves we very quickly ended up
    living a platonic lesbian life together.
She stayed over most nights. She stopped even asking if she could after
    a while.

She cleaned my house, we cooked together, we came up with our own
    favourite breakfast.
Croissant with chorizo, mozzarella, tomato, avocado and rocket.
Exact proportions sampled to perfection.
I made her packed lunches when she went home.
It was fucking cute.

She went in for revision surgery one day.
Just a small correction, in and out of hospital same day.
I came with, chatted to the nurses I'd just met a couple of months back.
She was in the room right next to where I was.
It was weird being a visitor.
I was able to snap out of the old post-op depression that I was warned
    about on my discharge notes.
'It's a big change in your life,' they said. 'Family rejection something-
    something, time to reflect, something.'
Either way, they were right.
But being in this place, remembering my hope for the future,
    willingness to fight...the love I felt for myself.
It was exactly what I needed.

She came out and everything was fine.
Of course, we checked out the surgeon's work right away.
I thought it looked great.
She wanted to walk around when it was obviously still inadvisable.
She can't sit still.
It's probs better she does that than sit and stress.
Stress is bad for healing.

She had a cigarette on the way to mine.

We've tried giving up cigarettes together but hey, these things are
    fucking addictive
and with what we have to put up with daily we really shouldn't be too
    hard on ourselves.

I nipped out for a counselling session right as we got home.
I talked to my counsellor about how much I like her,
about how frightened I am of feelings, of how I have no trust.
I talked about shared trauma and how we could even have sex with
    two bodies like ours.

I got back, we watched TV and got high.
I rested my head on her thigh, stroked her leg and felt her stroke my
    arm.
As we settled into bed, her lying next to me she said,
'I have feelings for you.'
I did too, so we kissed.

I thought her timing was immaculate.
Every time we kissed her clitoris bled a little.
Sometimes more than a little.
I thought it was hilarious.
I'd tease her and watch how pleasure would be followed by pain.
I'd flash her my vagina as I sat smoking a cigarette outside
or bite her on the back of her neck and ear.
Tension was building very fast.

She fucked me the next day,
then bled a lot.
It was fine, just too much excitement for the tiny bruised capillaries.

Grinding probs didn't help either.
Getting fucked was pretty amazing.
That was the first time anyone has touched me since I got a vagina.

We fucked again a few days later when she was a bit more healed and
*   no longer bleeding at the sight of me.*
This was her first time since surgery too.
There is an incredible amount of beauty in that.
Did I mention it was on the day of London Pride?

We fucked again the next day, on my sofa, in the light of a full moon.
Her fingers slid inside me, mine in her.
It was absolutely magical.
I never knew sex could feel that way.
When we were done I was buzzing, full of energy and couldn't sleep.
It was as if my whole body was made up of little smudges of light
It pulsed with energy and clarity.
Yeah, it was bloody magical.
That's the only way I can describe it.

And this happened even after I told her I had to make sure she was
*   real by tracing her relationship to my mother,*
- my own personal life hack -
When I'm in doubt, if there is someone who has met someone who has
*   met my mother, I know they're real.*
I figure since I came out of my mother she is as real as it gets so
*   anyone she can verify as real is real.*
Not the most reliable method seeing as my mum often sees things that
*   aren't real, but who cares.*
Anyway Casey, what I was trying to say, she thought that I was cute
*   even tho I'm a total weirdo.*

FROM GRINDER, WITH LOVE

Stephen

1.
Hi Mmm hot fella
You into plants
[Dick pic]

2.
U like getting sucked
*I do. You remember that I'm trans, yeah? Just
checking*
Yeh I no ur trans. But wat does it mean?

3.
So you got cock or pre op
Sorry a bit pissed

4.
And can I say you make a very handsome guy

5.
Does that mean u have the lady parts?
Well fucking hello to you too
Sorry to be rude
Just really curious
Sorry again

6.
Hi. You have a better beard than me lol

7.
So you are a trans?

8.
Got to admit gorgeous as a guy, stubble and tattoos. Curious.

9.
Hello
I always wanted to try pussy with ftm
I'm really scared lol never been with a female but turns me on

10.
Meaning you have a pussy?

11.
So you gay then?
Well yeah, why else would I be on here?
To do research
:D

WATER SIGNS

~~~~~~~

mud howard

i fell in love with a Scorpio, and somehow i am still, miraculously, alive. i'm a Cancer. which means i'm moody and guarded and feel most at home when i'm buying a Swiffer Wet Jet pack on Amazon. she is a Scorp. she is deep and intense and most at home when having entire weekends on vacation full of spiritual sex. she is an ocean, and i am her river. she is an alpha femme, witchy survivor, social top. i am a gender non-conforming ghoul. i don't know what i did to deserve her, but i know that i do.

we met in Oakland. a mutual friend put us in touch. some queer Australian babe that she and I had both individually gone on a date with years ago told her to contact me if she was travelling through San Francisco. all of a sudden, some hottie by the name of Princess was trying to add me on Facebook. i did my basic screening process. 1) is this person queer? 2) is this person cute? 3) do we have any friends in common?

the next day i got a message in my inbox from Princess saying that she was hoping to make it to the Bay. she wondered if i had any hot tips on what to see, whose couch she could crash on, or what queer or trans parties were on that weekend.

it was January. i had spent the whole month at the gym, listening to Rihanna's *Anti* album, getting acupuncture, staying up late nights drinking bone broth trying to thicken my blood before surgery. it was the type of month where the time stretches like saltwater taffy – where every morning is a countdown and every night is one sleep closer.

Princess was travelling the Cali coast with her friend from London. when my friends asked me what my plans were for the weekend, i told them i was hosting 'the Australians'. my American-ness was glaringly obvious. we made plans to meet up for dinner once i got off my shift at the transphobic coffee shop i still worked at.

we met at a Latin American place on Telegraph Ave. the walls were painted bright turquoise and pale pink, and it was Thursday. i walked up to the joint and saw two fierce femmes sitting outside at a small metal table smoking skinny cigarettes. they were both adorned in leopard print, all black everything, knee high Docs, fishnets and leather jackets, and giant gold hoop earrings dangling from their ears. i was so nervous while we waited in line to order our food. my mouth moved fast, full of words that didn't matter. my body temperature was rising under the weight of my denim vest and Princess's brown eyes.

i had a hard time understanding her accent. pro tip: don't ever confuse a Kiwi for an Aussie. she was from New Zealand: a land of green trees, white beaches and fierce indigenous resistance. i'm from America. a land of movies and new imperialism.

we got back to my apartment: a lower level duplex on 54th Ave. my roommates, a monogamish queer couple and their anxious dog, were out of town for the weekend at a cabin in Guerneville. i was set to drive up there the next day for Nash's birthday. we had the place to ourselves for the night. Princess and Chloe decided to make a run to the liquor store while i stayed home. i told them to surprise me with whatever alcohol they wanted. once they were gone, i made a carefully created shower playlist on the off chance that they would come home when i was still cleaning up. i had this visual that they would come back to the apartment, and i would walk out of the shower to Rihanna's 'Needed Me', in a cloak of steam, towel wrapped around my waist.

my fantasy was only troubled slightly by the fact that i was deeply out of sync with the current state of my body and couldn't bear to be naked in front of myself, let alone other people. my surgery was, at this point, only four days away. not only is it physically impossible to put a binder on in a humid room, but i also severely overestimated the amount of time it takes me to shower. in 10 minutes i was fully dressed, just standing around in the bathroom trying to busy myself before they came home. i scrubbed my tongue, plucked my eyebrows, applied layer after layer of mascara on my eyelashes. I kept peeking out the door every few minutes when i thought i heard a noise. eventually, I gave up on my suave shower entrance, and by the time they got back, i was, instead, posed on the futon in the lounge, reading a political book on kink.

we drank Salty Dogs and talked politics and the symbolism of high heels deep into the night. we ended up all hooking up that night. sometimes a threesome is the only socially acceptable thing to do, if you are a person who is even remotely sensitive to group dynamics. after we had successfully broken the tension by awkwardly fondling each other on the narrow futon, we agreed to go to sleep. after a brief check in, Princess and I headed off to one bed, while Chloe slept in the other.

the morning after was blue and starry. we lay in bed, two strangers hypnotised by the magnetic pull between us. i had to go to therapy and pick up my paycheck, so i chucked on a black sweatshirt and jeans and ventured out into the world.

before that night, i thought it would be impossible for me to have sex with anyone before my surgery. i had spent the past six months stumbling through the dark tunnel of dysphoria. i was never one of those kids who knew they were trans. i had never been in the 'wrong body', until boom, dysphoria put me in a headlock, six months on hormones. it was a bad scene. two months after moving to sunny California, i was trying on every shirt in my wardrobe, unable to get out of the house. i dyed my hair lavender. nothing helped. i spent all my free time on hold with Kaiser Permanente, listening to those weird air drums, correcting people on my deadname, and trying to escape everyone else's version of my gender.

i told my therapist that i was going to be celibate until the surgery. i couldn't imagine a scenario in which i'd be able to share my body with another person. i felt like sex was a risk i couldn't afford to take. i'd always been a very sexual person: letting boys feel me up in horror movies as a 13-year-old, loving the hot sweaty rush of hands on my body. even as an adult, i still wanked two, sometimes three times a day.

but now there was a part of my body that was no longer part of my body. that place was just a hunk of flesh, something that was numb and non-functional and heavy as concrete. every time someone misgendered me, i blamed it on my chest. sometimes i would be living my life, fully distracted and present, somehow separated from the gnarled root of my body tugging, and then my shoulders would slouch or stoop just a little, or i would stretch backwards, or someone else's eyes would hover for a second on the incongruence of my body, and suddenly i would evaporate from the moment. that's how dysphoria works. it steals you from yourself.

the summer before i moved, i slept with five people in a few weeks. one of those flings was with a self-proclaimed lesbian nature diva from Portland. how a lesbian can date a non-binary person who isn't and will never be a woman still confounds me. after 'hey girl'-ing me at my going away party a few times, she confessed to me outside that she didn't know how I conceptualised my gender. she said that she really liked boobs, and it was confusing for her whether or not i even liked mine or wanted her to touch them. after that, i had a hard time believing that the people i slept with wouldn't just use, or name or gender my body to match their own personal desires.

how could i share my body with someone else if it wasn't mine to share? i didn't even think it would be possible to make out with someone, if making out could lead to touching, tugging, pressing, fucking. even as a survivor, i didn't trust in myself enough to tell anyone not to touch me there. i figured i would wait it out. i would wait for the light switch of surgery to change my life for good and then hook up and fall in love with someone once i had healed. i wanted to be able to stand topless in the copper sun and give my body to the ocean, before i shared it with another person.

but there i was, enveloped in a palace of bedsheets and pillows with the hottest person i had ever met. the magnetism between our bodies was otherworldly. we wrestled and fucked and kissed the edges of each other's bodies, trying to suss out how deep we could go. i kept my shirt on the whole time we had sex. she never asked me to take my shirt off once. it didn't even come up. i don't know if you've ever had sex with any of your clothes still on, but at some point, that shit becomes an inferno. after a particularly hot moment, i was on top of her when she grabbed the bottom of my shirt from around my back and started fanning it back and forth to cool me down. that was when i knew this person was different.

after that weekend, i gave her a mix cd and we said goodbye. we didn't think we would see each other again. she gave me a ride to the airport and we made out in the backseat of the rental car like two teenagers, giggling and trying to sweet talk the security guards stalking around the 'No Stopping at Any Time' signs. i went back to Denver so my surgeon could make a new shape of me. she drove back to LA and hopped on a plane over the Atlantic back to London.

in the two weeks i was recovering from surgery we talked on the phone for at least eight hours every day. we talked moon signs, read *Argonauts* out loud to each other and had shy, extremely detailed phone sex. we talked about queer hierarchies in kink and poly, how *Titanic* was everyone's gay root, and how we both felt about our differing femme identities.

i kept thinking back to the astrology session i had with my woo astrologist Rosie Finn in Olympia the previous year. she kept saying that i was going to find somebody who was going *to rock my shit*. i had never been in a committed relationship with anyone before. i went from dating straight girls who had boyfriends to dating queer femmes who had partners. i had fallen in love many times: big purple streaks of passion flung across the sky, but nothing had stuck.

did i have commitment issues? was i too intense? was i lovable but only in small doses? was i destined for unequal relationships full of yearning and ghosted texts? was there some unwritten rule of being trans that meant i was too incongruent for anyone to truly understand? Rosie said no. she said i was going to meet someone who was going to make me say, *i need to be in a relationship with you.*

i lay in the basement bedroom of my parents' house, the room i grew up. i felt the electricity in my chest spasm and tingle as my body remembered itself. the nerve endings in my chest were fusing again, crawling all over each other in a wriggly pile of scar tissue. my chest was a numb expanse, but i couldn't remember a time when i felt more connected to it. here i was, lying in bed, hibernating in my childhood den, preparing to emerge back into my life, and there was this girl i knew nothing about, lying down on the other end of the phone, on the other side of the globe, asking if I had any plans to travel to London any time soon. two years later, and i live there.

EXPLORE ME

· · · · · · · · · · · · · · · ·

Caleb Murray

So. You wanna fuck me?
Well honey, that's fine by me.
Let's move things into the bedroom and go from there.
We fall to the bed, the passion and arousal building.
Our bodies a tangle of limbs, clothing and aggressive kisses.
The clothing begins to come off, shoes, socks, tops and trousers.
Clothes being flung to the other side of the room, disregarded.
We're down to our underwear now and our breath is heavy, faces
    flushed.
Hard kisses and bodies grinding. Your cock is hard and I'm wet.
You know what to expect before the underwear is taken off, what
    you're going to see.
Underwear is pulled off in a horny frenzy, leaving us completely nude.
Your eyes travel down my body with an aroused smile, until you reach
    my junk.
Then an oh so familiar expression creeps into your face. Oh shit.
Doubt appears in your eyes and you stop smiling.
You pull back and I can hear the questions forming.
'What do I do? How does it work? What if I don't like how it feels?'

I guide you gently back to the moment and try to reassure you.

Explain that I can talk you through it and you'll do fine.

But the doubt remains and I know you're uncomfortable. Out of your depth.

You're no longer hard and I'm no longer wet.

What was hot passion has gone cold. Arousal gone.

Confusion for you, frustration for me.

We chat some more, before you take your leave.

I curse softly before booting up a porn site.

See, I know why my body confuses people and makes people anxious.

My body defies what people think they understand.

That penis = man and vagina = woman.

Well I have both, but I'm not a man or a woman.

A surgically constructed penis and the vagina I was born with.

It's a bit of a mind fuck.

But you see, it's why I tell people. To try and avoid this.

Avoid the identity crisis from insecure cis men.

Avoid the inevitable result.

If people can't handle my body, that's just fine.

But please don't say you can and then waste my time.

I have desires.

I have needs.

I want them met by someone who will take the challenge.

Treat my body as an adventure, as something to be met with excitement.

Discover pleasures and sensitive spots which neither of us expect.

Give in to passion, lust and red-hot arousal.

If you want to take that adventure, you only need to ask.

Because you never know, I might just say yes.

'AS THOUGH IT WERE EASY'

~~~~~~~

Faith DaBrooke

Edward was late and that made me a little hopeful that he was going to stand me up and leave me sitting here at the bar, sipping on a gin and tonic, all alone. It wouldn't be a bad thing if he didn't show, not entirely bad at least. Lolita was a cute bar. It was dim enough with a few Christmas lights and votive candles to add a little glow. There was exposed brick, dark wood furnishings and a clean scent that made it more comfortable than the nearby dives and Irish pubs I generally frequented. There was a little back room, a few stools at the bar, and me with my new curly, dark wig, a black A-line dress with a deep scoop neck and layered lace. My nails were dark red and matched my lip color. I'd done my best with a smokey eye tutorial I'd found online.

I hoped that I looked beautiful, sitting there at the bar, cross legged in my black heels and lace, a blood red smear of lipstick on my half drunk cocktail. I felt beautiful, though I was starting to doubt my judgement. Why had I agreed to go on a date tonight with a guy? I could feel all my nerves ball up in my stomach and I felt as if I had stepped outside my own body. My hands were shaking a little bit. Maybe he wouldn't show up.

In anticipation, I had gone and got my first manicure, which had been a thoroughly awkward experience. My unfamiliarity with the practice, something I assume my mother or sorority sisters were supposed to have outlined for me, certainly didn't help. Not only was I unaware that you were supposed to pick out your own polish color at the start but I lost most of my pinkie nail when the woman just started cutting my nails without even asking. Apparently, you have to say you want them long. It also took me quite a long time to figure out the whole square nails versus round nails, partly because there was a language gap, but also because the woman was quiet and mumbled a little. Not knowing the difference, I just said 'round' and went with it.

The other thing no one mentioned is that you're supposed to bring cash for the tip even if there are little credit card stickers on the door. This necessitated a post-manicure run over to the grocery to buy some gummy bears so I could get cash back and tip. Plus there's no indication of when you're done on the little hand dryer because I kept seeing women there hitting the fan button over and over again. But in the end my nails looked amazing – long, perfectly feminine, and fierce in dark crimson. So I guess it was all worth it. Even the parts where I had to hold hands with a stranger.

All along the walk home I kept looking at my nails, holding them up and moving them a little like I was some hippie on acid. Having my nails professionally done felt so much girlier than doing them myself. And they looked way nicer, especially on my right hand since I'd never mastered leftie nail polish application.

After I got home, I took a long bubble bath and carefully shaved every last inch of my body before loofaing with apricot and strawberry body wash that basically smelled like candy. Then I dried off, lotioned up, shaved my face a good two or three times in every direction, carefully put on my makeup, and got dressed. Though it was September and beginning to cool down a little, I still blasted the air conditioning on high. The last thing I wanted to do was sweat and ruin my artfully applied makeup. The eyeshadow alone had taken me a good 20 minutes.

Earlier in the week I'd gone wig shopping after work. After doing some research on the internet, I had found a huge wig shop near 34th Street. A reviewer had raved about its selection and the photos I'd seen online looked impressive. I'd decided that I would try a lace-front wig, which was supposed to look more natural. As I was going for natural, I picked out a chestnut brown that more or less matched my natural hair color. It was a natural and synthetic blend and cost a little more than I wanted to spend but seemed worth it. It was a little longer than shoulder length, straight at the top then slowly melting into perfect, wonderful curls at the bottom. When the clerk asked if I wanted them to cut the lace for me I heartily agreed, even if it was an extra five dollars. While I'd read about how to cut the lace, the last thing I wanted to do was ruin the wig before I even put it on.

Fully dressed and with my makeup set, I then put on my necklace; a delicate silver chain with a tiny silver heart pendant. It took me five frustrating minutes to try and chain it behind my head before I gave up and used a safety pin. Then I put in my earrings – silver hoops just over an inch in diameter. The last thing I wanted to do was mess up my hair trying to put jewelry on. To round it out I added a couple of rings and a bracelet, also silver.

In my mind, accessories helped you pass better. Lots of accessories meant you hadn't just picked up a dress at the thrift shop and thrown it on. No, they meant you had a lifetime of collecting little bits and bobs. For the same reason, I always carefully made sure to have the right amount of junk in my purse – a pen, receipts, mints, extra hair bands and even a couple of tampons.

With everything in its place, I only had the wig left. I pulled it out of the plastic, then out of the net, pulled off the flimsy little plastic crown, removed the cardboard supports, and placed it on my head. I shifted it around trying to get the right angle and finally found it with the parting slightly off center. I couldn't help but smile at how natural it looked, almost as if it were my own hair. I pulled a few strands back into a clip because having a hair clip also helped with passing. It meant you didn't just throw on a wig, you had actual hair that needed to be styled and held in place with products you had purchased in your ordinary life. Looking in the mirror I didn't feel ordinary though. I felt beautiful.

I spritzed perfume in the air and then walked through the cloud like I had seen people do on TV. Then, just to be sure, I also sprayed a tiny bit on my wrists and neck. Lastly, I double checked that all the right stuff was in my purse – keys, wallet, phone, lipstick and gloss, a compact, and my little point-and-shoot camera in case the opportunity for photos presented itself. I also grabbed a black cardigan and draped it over my arm as I stepped into my patent black heels. Before I left the house, I stopped in front of the mirror to look myself over. My clothes were perfect. My makeup was perfect. My hair was perfect. I had probably done too much perfume but it would wear off. I breathed out slowly and tried to shake off my nerves. I was doing this. I was really doing this. I was a beautiful girl going out for a night on the town.

Maybe he wouldn't show. Then I could enjoy a night as a pretty girl out in a bar. Maybe some other person would buy me drinks and tell me how beautiful I was. Maybe I could go home and forget that I had stupidly agreed to go out on a date with a guy. I had only wanted to feel like a regular, normal, everyday girl and it had seemed like a fun idea when he had asked. Now cold panic coursed through my veins and I downed the rest of my drink as quickly as I could. Maybe he wouldn't show up. I checked my phone and he was already eight minutes late. Maybe he was standing me up and I wouldn't make a complete fool of myself. Then I caught myself looking up at the door. Of course, he showed up.

* * *

Luckily, Edward was tall, taller even than I was in heels. That was part of the reason I had agreed to go out with him. Tonight, he was wearing nice jeans – nicer than any pair that I owned – and a dark brown sweater that fitted his fit torso perfectly in a way that none of my guy clothes ever seemed to. Even his shoes were nice. They weren't sneakers but some well-polished dress shoes. His hair was dark brown, nicely cut, and recently razored on the edges of the back and sides. He was clean shaven with just a hint of lotion scent left on him. He had pale skin too, though it had seen more sun than mine, and he had expressive brown eyes that squinted shut when he laughed. Edward was cuter than me; cuter than Matt. As Sarah, I felt as if I could jump up a league or two.

Seriously, I'd have to say that Sarah is way out of my league and that's such a weird thing when you think about it. Heck, Sarah probably wouldn't even talk to me or would at least dismiss me in a nice enough way before going about her business. And this isn't even my judgement. She gets a 9.8 on Hot-or-Not, while I think as a guy I managed only a respectable 7 or 8. It's such a weird superpower to have.

'So what type of art do they have at your gallery?' he asked, taking a sip of his beer and giving me a cool smile. I sort of wished I could have a have a beer too. After all, the bar had a decent selection. But on account of Edward and I both being guys and me being the pretend girl, it was best to keep my drinks as feminine as possible. The more contrast I could draw between me and Edward the better. Already I'd graduated from gin and tonic to vodka cranberry.

'Oh,' I said, trying to keep my voice on target. 'It's not really a gallery. I mean, we have art on the wall but no one ever buys it.' I wasn't on target. If a perfect female voice was the target then I kept accidentally winging gay men and valley girls.

'I'd love to see it sometime though, it sounds cool.' Smiling, he kept eye contact and I felt his hand on knee. It wasn't moving or caressing, but sitting there on my knee, a tiny bit above my knee on the lowest part of the thigh, not the sexy part of the thigh, just the lower part of the thigh. How does one react to a hand on the leg? Eighteen years of school, four years of college, and no one ever taught me how to react if a dude put his hand on my bare leg. Maybe they covered it in girls' gym class. Do you move it off? Say something? Instead, I did nothing and ignored it. I pretended that nothing was happening at all. We were two people having an ordinary conversation like you would with your boss or your great aunt.

'It's nothing special,' I said, accidentally catching myself making eye contact. It was inescapable. Edward was casually turned toward me, one elbow on the bar to manage his drink, his other hand on the smooth skin of my leg. I was frozen like a statue. Any move

I made could potentially signal awareness of the presence of his hand. As rigidly as I could I sat there, took a sip of my icy pink drink, turned back to him and accidentally made eye contact again. Nervously I smiled as I tried to think of something other than me to talk about. 'What about your job? It sounds a lot more exciting.'

It didn't sound exciting all but I didn't know what else to say. Edward was a dental hygienist. Who enjoys talking about dentistry? Personally, I hated being at the dentist; lying back in that chair and staring up at the bright light while your mouth is filled with odd, horrifying equipment. It's not all that different from what alien abductees report, minus any genital stuff or anal probing anyway. Simply thinking about the dentist sent nervous shivers up my spine, fingernails scratching up the blackboard of my soul. Why did I ask him about dentistry?

'Well for one thing people always lie about flossing,' he chuckled. 'You know, we look at teeth all day. We can tell if you're lying.'

'What do you do when people lie?' I asked. 'Do you, like, call people out?'

'No, not like that.'

'I have something to confess,' I said with a coy smile. 'I don't floss.'

'You really should. It's important,' he replied without a hint of irony. Instinctively, I stopped smiling and closed my lips. I think he was looking at my teeth.

It had been fun to chat with him online. It had been fun to even be flirty with him online. This was all my fault really. He had sent me a message one day and it happened to be one of the days I was drunkenly interneting. So I wrote back and we started chatting on instant messenger. He was friendly, he was funny, and best of all he had managed to not be the least bit creepy. Sure, it still made me cringe a tiny bit when he complimented me and called me beautiful, or especially sexy, but unlike other guys who wrote to me, Edward could form a sentence, use a spellchecker and write in non-caps. He'd never asked me too many personal questions about being a boy or about my genitals. Even better he had never once mentioned his cock, nor had he sent me photos of it. Then after a few weeks of pretty frequent chatting, he asked me to meet him for happy hour.

'Sure, let's do that some time,' I'd replied via chat, carefully leaving the day and time as vague as possible. Maybe tomorrow. Maybe 25 years from now. A part of me was fascinated with the idea of it. I could even take off work so I could get dressed up, meet him at 5:30pm and lie about how I had just come from the office. I'd even sort of lie to myself and imagine I'd gone to work that day as a woman, walked around Manhattan, ridden the subway at rush hour, waited for my sandwich at the deli – all those normal things a professional would do. Plus going on a date with a guy was definitely on my gender exploration bucket list.

There were a few things on that list, including going to the beach in a bikini, wearing a sparkly slinky gown to a black-tie event, wearing a dress on a boat and feeling the breeze, going on vacation to another town, and bringing only women's clothing with me so I'd be forced to spend the entire time as a girl. And going on a date with a guy was on there too. I liked girls. I'd always liked girls but there was something to the idea of going out with a guy, something that made me feel feminine in a way that makeup and dresses didn't. It was a new feminine feeling that twisted in my belly and flooded my brain with many different interesting chemicals.

So when my computer beeped that familiar little instant

messenger sound, I saw that Edward had promptly written back 'How's Thursday? Lolita bar? 6:30pm? :)'

'Yes,' I'd written and it was only after I'd hit enter that the panic started to grip me. Still, things don't take themselves off your bucket list. You have to push through the panic and do it, even if you're not quite sure what you're doing.

* * *

It was dark on the Lower East Side but there were still plenty of people on the street, even after nine on a weeknight. We left the bar and headed up Allen past stores with Chinese signs where tired looking young Chinese men were unloading boxes of foul smelling food from unmarked minivans. We walked by groups of old, beaten-up looking men, standing around in groups smoking outside a halfway house. Having Edward with me made me feel a little safer as we passed them. I let myself drift closer to him. Outside a coffee shop, a homeless guy, his nearby shopping cart filled to the brim with old luggage and bags, stood to attention at the door, ready to open it for customers and hoping for a little bit of change in exchange for this mostly unwanted service. As we strolled past shuttered and gated art galleries and stores, I felt Edward take my hand.

It wasn't too hot out or too cold of a night. It was one of those perfect New York nights you get maybe five times a year if you're lucky. Apparently neither the Dutch settlers, nor the Lenape Indians, nor the Chinese immigrants, nor halfway house residents, nor the suburban expats like me were all that concerned about living somewhere with decent weather. I liked good weather because it was fun to wear dresses in good weather. You didn't need tights or boots like in winter and you didn't have to worry about your hand being too sweaty if someone tried to hold it.

Though I didn't want to lead him on, I let him hold my hand and we walked together, Edward put his hand around my shoulder and I even let myself feel happy. I was happy he wasn't talking about dentistry or baseball but mostly happy that he was treating me like a girl. Mentally, I checked this item off my list and bit my lip a little, wondering if this was really what it felt like to be someone's girl or whether this was still somehow an ersatz version of the genuine feeling. Did I really like him? What if he was in love with me? Was I leading him on, using him as a pawn in my own quest for female experiences? Maybe he was a willing pawn.

'You sure you don't want to go for dinner?' he asked. 'I know a really good French bistro near here. You'd like it. It's romantic.'

'No, I should go,' I said sadly. It was true.

'What about ice cream?' he kept pleading, a little bit of worry in his voice. 'No one can say no to ice cream.'

'I have work in the morning,' I said, plus this was potentially dangerous and I knew it. What if Edward felt led on? What if he felt as if he deserved something from me, something I didn't want to give? He was bigger than me and he worked out too. And I worried that I would do something silly like get drunk and let him kiss me. No, drinks were enough.

'I guess I can take the F to 34th and transfer there,' I said, knowing there was an F somewhere nearby. Normally I hated transferring trains, but otherwise I'd have to walk all the way over to Prince to catch the R. Being from Astoria and working in Tribeca, I knew of the J, M and Z trains but they were mostly a mystery to me.

'Okay,' he said reluctantly and we silently walked back towards Delancy. Outside the subway station it was brighter and busier. The darkness of the streets gave way to the light of the avenue. We paused for a moment and I turned to face him.

'Thank you for the drinks, Edward,' I said with a little half smile. 'I had a good time.'

'Me too,' he said and I felt his hand slide around my waist as he leaned in and kissed me. A kiss was fine, I could manage a kiss. A kiss was the perfect way to end the night. Then I felt his tongue in my mouth and like the hand on my leg, I didn't know what to do. Should I pull away or let him kiss me? Do I kiss him back? Not wanting to be weird or make a scene I kissed him back. We stood there on that Manhattan street, on the Lower East Side and kissed. I was making out with him. I was making out with a guy. Other than the slight scratch of his beard on my skin it wasn't physically any different from kissing a girl. Despite the binding, despite the fact that I'd never been attracted to guys, I could feel a throb between my legs as blood rushed down. I did my best to remind myself that it was nothing but a physiological response. That was all. It wasn't arousal. I wasn't getting turned on. I was a girl doing what girls do on nights out with a boy. That was all. I was in a role, playing my part in a rather intimate theatrical performance.

"'You're so beautiful, Sarah,' he said as I broke it off. For a moment we stood there on the sidewalk by the stairs down to the B/D on Grand. Even with my heels he was taller than me. We stood close, Edward with his hands around my waist, me with one hand on his chest and my other on his side just above his belt. Whatever I had been trying to do worked. There on the street with Edward, my lips still tasting his, my lipstick no doubt smeared to hell, I felt like a girl, like a real live honest to God girl out living her life.

'Thank you,' I said quietly, not bothering to look away and letting our eyes meet. Here was a guy who treated me like an ordinary girl, not like some t-girl fetish object, but like a regular, ordinary girl out on a night with her guy. A thought gently floated through my mind. Should I go and have dinner, ice cream, another vodka cranberry? Should I stick with this and see where the night went? A warm feeling swelled in my stomach and I felt almost light headed. Was I being too hasty in ending our night?

'I can't wait to suck your cock,' he said in what he probably thought was a sexy voice.

'Yeah, so...,' I offered, trying to think of what to say. 'I think I have to go.' Slipping away, out of his arms, I let the gentle smile slide from my face and I gave him a little wave. 'Have a good night,' I called back as I made my way quickly down the stairs. Already I could hear the train rumbling and at this hour I didn't want to miss it. Maybe I should leave the guys to the straight girls.

LAST NIGHT

. . . .

Grace E. Reynolds

i found out
that rejection
is a loaded gun
and i am alive
because you couldn't
quite get me
to put
the barrel
in my mouth

STAR-CROSSED

~~~

Sid S. Coles

Love says, 'I'm new at this.'

'It's new to me too,' I say, having moved for decades in the constellation of *Saphos clarus* – femmes, bois, dykes, lesbians, androgenes. Until you.

After a few sincere attempts to remain hygienic, you finally negotiate your exit from a 25-year het marriage.

We spend weeks barely sleeping. You've never had sex in five-hour stints before. We fall asleep cunt-plumbed and smiling; legs and fingers knotted, hair matted to our foreheads and pubic bones.

In your journal, you write, '*I see brilliant colours upon ignition; on skin, on clit, on tongue: silver; ochre, the vibrant blue that swifts up flame.*'

You paint yourself, full lipped, acorn-hat-topped into spiral poems. Words that swallow words. *Poemaintings*, you call them. From painting to painting, you transform from snail, to dog, to seal, to lion among words that eat themselves. The word *ouroboros* never comes up.

Midway into March I go in for a number 3 short back and sides and donate my few remaining dresses and skirts.

At a summer patio on College Street you set your Negroni glass down and worry.

'I don't know what to do when gay guys flirt with you, when straight men fumble, when women blush. Eros whirls around you. I feel dwarfed by it.'

And later you text, 'Your otherness is like a dark star; enigmatic and vivid around the edges. There is a vortex of degeneracy at its centre that breaks down, emulsifies the particulates of convention and confuses the fuck out of me. I have never walked beside a black star before.'

From Wikipedia:[1] *A black star need not have an event horizon, and may or may not be a transitional phase between a collapsing star and a singularity.*

In the fall, I start talking about surgery; the event horizon. Your crescent smile wanes.

We find my new name together. As soon as you say it I feel as if I have been hurtling towards 'Sidney' forever.

'Am I still a lesbian if you transition? Everywhere we go, you'll be read as a guy. I'm so confused.'

'Your identity isn't a hostage to mine,' I say. 'Who I am is not who you are and my becoming is not yours.'

You fret.

As it nears, it occurs to me that the event horizon may mark

---

1   Wikipedia – https://en.wikipedia.org/wiki/Black_star_(semiclassical_gravity).

the end of us and that love may not survive this particular reconfiguring of a sometimes night-sky.

Best not to constellate or name things. Fixty, we decide, coaxes the eye to blindness.

You text me a quote from the book you're reading. There are stars on its cover.

'May I only ever glimpse you, and you me,' I text back.

'Perfect,' says Love.

FUCKING FEELINGS

~~~~~~~~

Freiya Benson

Sometimes I wonder what I'm doing.

I just stop and look at the mess around me, and the way that emotions make me feel, and I wonder why I keep on doing it.

Sometimes I wish that you actually could burn out the emotions that happen when something good doesn't work out. Sometimes I'd like to not feel, to not have that grip around my heart, that empty feeling in the pit of my stomach.

I'd really like to be able to eat something without wanting to immediately throw it right back up. I'd really like to feel that I want to eat at all.

And yet, in the moment, oh my god, in the moment, that sense, that rush, that swell of emotion that engulfs me when I drop my guard and let myself feel. How could I give that up?

It's like a drug, and I know I'm addicted.

The sense of belonging, even for just a while, is something I need. Walking along the seafront at five in the morning, your arm round my waist, mine around yours, the smell of your hair as it occasionally blows into my face, how could I want to forget that?

And yet now, when I see that's likely the only time I'll know that moment with you, there's a part of me that almost wishes it wasn't real. The sadness of knowing that's all there ever will be is crushing, and that pain, that's something I wish I didn't have. That's something that never changes.

My problem is that I feel. All of our problems are that we feel. Feelings are the worst, and yet, I keep on doing them. We keep on doing them.

When we kissed, you said you don't do feelings. You told me that I make you feel, and I told you that maybe just for now, right at this moment, feelings are okay. They needn't last forever, they can just be about the moment.

I was right, but I was also wrong. Feelings start in the moment, but they don't always stop there. Sometimes they carry on, and they follow you around, like a shadow you can't see, always a little behind you, but there nonetheless.

Fucking feelings. They eat me up, and stop me from being okay.

And I don't know what to do with them. I don't know where to put them when they become memories. I don't know how to feel about how to feel.

Friends tell me that I need to protect myself better, to develop a tougher exterior, but I don't want to harden up. I don't want to build a shell to protect myself, even though it would be the sensible thing to do. I'm afraid that if I do, it'll make me cold. I'm afraid that I'll no longer be able to feel anything at all. And yet I know the stark truth in this, as if I didn't feel then I wouldn't have to spend days, weeks, months getting over people, and I wouldn't feel that sadness that walks alongside me in those times.

But I'm afraid of losing the ability to feel, just the same. Like I said before, it's a drug.

I leaned in close to your ear and asked if I could kiss you. You leaned in as well, and as our lips touched I felt the rushing of blood through my body, the tingling of nerve endings, the softness of your mouth, and the gentle warmth of your tongue as it discovered mine. It felt like everything else dissolved away, even though we were surrounded by a hundred other people, and the music was so loud.

Your hand touches my face, and as we kiss you slowly stroke my cheek. My skin prickles with goosebumps, but it's not from the sharpness of the winter night.

My god, those feelings. They run rampant through my soul and make me realise that this is what life is about. Connections and emotions. Links between people, delicate and strong, like spider silk, weaving lives together, sometimes fleetingly, sometimes forever.

Those glorious, burning, heart-ripping feelings.

And we can never win. It's like a glacier, a huge, unrelenting, emotional glacier. We chip away at its vast hulk, trying to get a foothold while all the while it keeps on coming.

We can climb to the top, only to look around and realise it's so vast, so uncharted, that we were foolish to even think we could ever claim it as ours alone.

I need to feel, even when I don't want to feel. I need to know what it is to keep the glacier at bay. I need the warmth from another, I need the warmth from you.

I know that given time I'll forget what this feels like. I know this because when I do feel like this I remember the times it's happened before. I remember the feelings, the magnificent, all-consuming intense and beautiful feelings. I remember all the feelings, even the gut-wrenching, all-engulfing, salty sharp feelings.

The happiness, the sadness, and everything that lives in the gaps between.

Sometimes I wonder what I'm doing.

Then I remember, and I realise that even if I could, I'd never give this up. How could I ever let go of those glorious, burning, heart-fucking feelings?

How could I even think that was an option?

REAL

~~~~~~~~~

Deeana Violet

She turns and looks at me. She's sitting on a bench outside the club. Black hair in two massive, impossible bunches. Makeup like a cartoon barbarian. She smiles at me and I fall in love instantly. She's not in the slightest bit real and I've dreamed about her since I was five years old. I love her with every single fragment of me (and there's a lot of fragments, believe it, I've glued myself back together a lot). I know she comes to tell me something. I don't know what it is.

Yeah. Keep telling yourself that.

Decades. Are you lucky enough to have a life that you can measure in decades, to have life experience that long? To be able to say, 'Oh, that was 30 years ago'? Decades. Glacial time. Nearly get married. Fail at it. Nearly get married again and start smoking because you know that it doesn't matter if you die young, because that would be preferable to living like this.

People around me joke about it. About lipstick and lingerie and *dressing up for fun* and I freeze because I'm the one you apologise to if you make a sex joke. The look of terror on my face must be a picture. Never fails to kill the mood. I freeze, which is ironic, because something inside me is cracking like ice over dark water.

Sitting with her on a hillside, crammed together on a wooden bench, looking down over hazy meadows, the world perfected. She's so beautiful. I never feel this alive when I'm awake. The sun is setting; it's like getting lost in someone's art. She looks at me, afraid suddenly.

'You know I was a man, right?'

I suddenly do know, and I don't care at all. When I awake, I cry tears that are thick and bitter, like something broke deep in my head.

My every instinct suppressed by years of horror. The Great Fear in a Northern town. Stones in the street, thrown because *they* could tell it was a blouse, even if my parents couldn't. Grew a beard. Without it, I looked like a starlet. Too scared to admit to that, to how much I wanted to love that face, so I hid it away from the world for 20 years, I think. The ingénue is long gone, sad to say, but I quite like the face I shaped in her memory.

And I walked on and on and on through the days, one second at a time, one step. Until the days came when I was able to learn some of the faces of love. The face of a love, so close to mine, plucking my eyebrows, taking me makeup shopping for the first time. A fierce love, bound and patterned with scars of all shapes, uncompromising, blazing. Calls me *she* and my heart leaps. Beyond any definition. Lover, friend, partner, ex, none of them remotely what we are. Their gender so scattered to the wind too. Other loves, holding my hand in the street, barely dressed, heels click on the pavement, cheap shit cardboard coffee, huge shades, a nylon wig to die for. Accepting, dark eyes and fierce, perfect laughter against the things I'd feared; another face, flaming hair and utter uncompromising devotion to freedom. All my people, so many more than these. Lending me their strength until I had my own.

I don't want labels for my people. I gave up monogamy when I gave up masculinity. Each person, each connection bringing something new, and that feeling of changing and shifting. Fluid and no longer bonded to any form, to anything other than my own ethics and morality. To rewrite and reclaim everything. To reclaim the act of fucking; to be able to shrug and say, *nah, don't tend to like my dick getting involved, you fancy scratching my back up a bit instead?* To be able to say that and be understood, as though it's not even anything worth noting, except as a preference? How can you not love every partner, right there, in the moment? That feeling that builds until every muscle is bursting with love, of them, of that place, that moment, this life, this freedom, this form? To love freely and with honesty and integrity. Worth dying for, worth dying for a thousand times.

I held her close.
She was still there when I woke.

POEMS

. . . .

Alex Ahmed

i. Every day

I love you less, I want to say
Less every day like with every
strand of hair falling out or every
dead cell becoming dust
collecting where the walls meet the floor
and in the rug and in the hidden corners I don't clean
until I do, and I want to say
how did all this come out of me?

ii. Language

Loving you is
My first language
And I've only practised Losing you
On Duolingo for like two weeks
I can barely say the word goodbye
It just doesn't
Sound right

iii. *The whole of the earth*

I felt light like
I was a weight being lifted off
By your energy
I felt life like
I never had before
When I saw the whole of the earth
In an eyeful
I felt light like
I'm closer to the sun than I've ever been
And colder still
When the whole of the earth
Is behind me

iv. 'Consider different fading systems'

I'm the mote you breathed in, benign
and I took residence among your cells
and capillaries and veins leading to your heart
there I felt your heat, your laughter
booming, shaking and throwing me around your cells
and capillaries and veins leading to your heart
there I felt your breathing slow
to a gentle rocking
and I found a way inside your cells
and capillaries and veins
leading to your heart

v. Fallen

You're the first snow's
fresh fallen kiss

made melting tear
and always mist

vi. Traces
I traced the water by the ending of the lights
And the morning by the ending of the night
And the contours of the cave I'd carved
Deep in my heart
By what we have left

vii. Light
There was a time
before the lights went out
when I worried I'd forget what light was
There was a time
before the lights went out
when there was nothing I wanted so badly
I wanted to keep them on until morning
and after that until it was night again
and after that until everything burned out
anything so I wouldn't have to adjust
And there was a time
long after the lights went out
when I felt like I could see.

SOMEONE I LOVE IS TRANS

L-J

Someone I love is trans. I love her and she loves me, and it's the healthiest, most balanced, nourishing and gloriously loving relationship I have ever had. It's the one I've been waiting for, the one that fits into place, that makes me realise how relationships should be. She's, well, she's the one.

I love her in all the huge and tiny ways that love surprises you.

I love her slender back, shaped like a pale violin, her slim hips that wear jeans like jeans were meant to be worn. I love her long graceful arms; how she moves them like an ecstatic swan when she dances round the room in her socks singing a joyful song of love for a snack she's eating, a comic she's bought, or the cuteness of my (our!) cat. I love the funny words she uses and how she insists on getting them wrong, bending them to the will of her humour like brightly coloured elastic tools she's found to describe her vision of the world. I love that she won't sleep without her bear and that she loves building fires and planting trees. I love that she wears pink penguin-covered pyjamas and that she'll take all the spiders out of our room.

And there are the ways I love her because she is trans. The things I see and the things I have learned to see.

I love her when I notice her inspecting her body in the mirror, admiring her curves and her long hair, the shapes that make her a woman. That slender back, those slim hips and long arms of her tall body that sometimes betrays her in the eyes of others.

So because I love her, sometimes I'll take her home a few pairs of new socks that, you know, I've just picked up in town for her because they're colourful and cute. But really, it's because I know she needs some and she would have had to buy them in the wrong clothing section to get the ones that fit. I can take away those ten minutes of pain because, the way life's die fell, I can just go and buy socks wherever I please.

I love her when we go on holiday to shared adventures in foreign lands, am lifted by the joy she finds in the smallest details along the way and the beautiful images she captures of them.

So because I love her I stay close by in the airport security queues, to be on hand should they question her passport or, god forbid, please no, never let this happen, decide to put her in the body scanner.

I love that she has one of those bodies that looks great in everything she wears, tall and Amazonian and beautiful.

So because I love her I stare down the attendant by the changing rooms in clothes shops, just daring them to challenge her or make her feel uncomfortable for going in to try on a cute top.

She has one of those bodies that means danger, that people want to expose as a trick, a threat, a target to somehow score smug points by pointing it out as a lie.

So because I love her, I stare a lot of people down.

In the street, in restaurants, on trains and at bus stops, I step in front, go through first, do the talking, and I meet their stare and I glare, screaming at them with my eyes to stop looking that bit too long and just you fucking dare say a word or you'll have to go through me. I have a good hard stare and poor eyesight, a few defended issues and quite a lot of anger of my own, so fortunately scowling fiercely at people comes pretty easy. Allegedly, I've been scowling since I was a child, maybe in training so sometimes I can love her against the world? And in the moment, it works, on the surface anyway. People might not learn or change their views right there, but they do learn that it feels uncomfortable to be the focus of someone's stare and they look away, caught in their ignorant act.

And even though I love her nine times round the sun, it's not always enough.

It's not enough when sometimes I get it wrong and it's me who hurts her; maybe I ask the wrong question on the wrong day, or I shout at that person in the street whose head turns, whose eyes swivel, that person she hadn't noticed because she's learned not to see it all so that she can navigate the streets, and I blow that cover with my challenge and it ruins her day, not theirs.

And all the love in the world is not enough when she can't function for a week because someone has devastated her by misgendering her. When they thoughtlessly pull her whole sense of identity down around her in ashen ruins with one tiny word, one syllable of ignorance or hate, 'mate'. When she can't get out of bed, when she can't face the world, when she just can't see how to get through the rest of forever because this is never going to go away and there will always be someone who will rob her of her core. When that someone is her parent.

I am a partner and I am an ally, so I stand up where I can with my love and my stare and my care.

Yet the world expects me to abide by my privilege. Expects me to 'tell' them about her. To spare them perhaps a second of discomfort, protect their *cis*comfort, when they wonder whether my girlfriend is *really* a girl, whether they should greet her with a kiss or shake her hand firmly and pat her on the back for her bravery and perhaps their (in)security. I will gladly wield whichever words and weapons will help fight her battles, because I love this woman in my life, who happens to be trans.

ON LOVE – WHAT ARE YOU THINKING ABOUT LOVE RIGHT NOW?

I am filled by love. Buoyed by it.

I'd love it if there were more love in my live.

I think in the past I did often fall in love, but only now I have the freedom to experience love. Or at least I learned to allow this freedom.

I have a lot to give. I long for the warmth of someone loving me living close by – romantically or also as friends; family (parents etc.) isn't really enough these days, although it gives me plenty of love.

I'm thinking the world needs more of it, and I'm thinking that it starts with loving ourselves enough to risk really loving others in an open and mutual way.

That not many people in my life deserve my love.

That I'll never find a partner because I come with too much baggage, a large portion of that because of being trans/non-binary.

I feel that at this point in my life I have finally started to get a handle on love, in the sense that I know what I want and perhaps more importantly, what I don't want. I feel confident enough that I can and will have a fulfilling and happy life if I choose not to have partners and this has given me the wherewithal to strive to commit to being as honest and transparent as I can with myself and with people to whom I am attracted. Right now, I feel very drawn to wanting to make connections with other trans women. I want to have sex but most importantly I want to find friendship. I want the women in my life to know how much I love and value them and I want the time that we spend together to feel like healing and nurturing. Perhaps for the first time in my life I'm entertaining the idea that non-monogamy might be something which could work for me. I fall in love so easily.

Love scares me right now. I hope that in the future I'll feel less like a blob of exposed flesh and more able to accept love and relationships.

It keeps me going. It is a lifeline for me. When I feel at my lowest points my partner's love and reassurance pulls me through.

That it's incredible how I have one human being on earth who so completely understands me and that I find it difficult to even comprehend what would happen if I didn't have her. In a very practical sense, how could I ever call it love with anyone else who doesn't actually know me as well as she does? Wouldn't I just get irritated with them because I'd have to explain every single reference I made?

Painful and unobtainable.

I miss my love dearly.

I'm thinking I'm going to wake up my bf with sex when I get back.

Meh humph.

Love is troublesome at the best of times and devastating at others.

It's a mutual admiration and respect between two or more close beings. It takes many forms. It doesn't last forever, although it feels as if it will at the time. It makes me both happy and sad.

Love is difficult and painful, but also beautiful. It can make you feel more alive than you've ever felt, or crush you. You can't get one side without the other, and it's something that needs to be balanced. Although my love is hurting now, I know that in the end it will be okay. I know I will move past the pain and find a peace and comfort.

Love needs to be liberated from love.

I actually had to go to a (straight) wedding over the holiday period, something I usually avoid, but the invitation came from a unique friendship. Sitting in the church (I avoid weddings for religious as well as cishetnorm reasons), I found myself thinking instead about revolution. That making a commitment to being open and vulnerable, to sharing and trusting, to generating energy for a future makes change. Or rather, that that's how I want to think about love, rather than as some kind of end-stopped, self-satisfied pair-bonding. When I think about the lovers who've inspired me (my lovers, other people who love), it's because they invited me to think about sustaining changes towards openness, and an openness towards change. That's being tested in my current (long-term, dyadic) relationship right now as I go public about being non-binary, but we are using words like 'adventure' to think about how a profound change for me can be something that happens together. I'm thinking that I need to think a lot about love, that love – including of non-human beings, of the planet, even of art – is something done through the mindbody, and as I redefine or rethink my mindbody, I might do love differently, or understand it differently. Maybe less diffidently, maybe I will be more able to believe that I am worthy of love rather than having to earn it or perform for it.

I'm in love with someone who makes me feel like the best version of myself and who makes me feel as if I can be myself. Love is what is giving me strength right now, to find a job and to find friends.

I'm optimistic about it and happy with my love life. I feel as if love transcends physical form.

That it is essential, but infinite; that it is a part of me and there's no need to worry about it.

Love is showing your vulnerabilities to others. I may appear confident and capable, self-assured and strong, but these are just the doors I close to stop people getting close. I pretend I like doing stuff on my own. I act as if I'm doing it because I'm cool, or I don't actually need anybody, as if I've been doing this for so long that it really doesn't matter anyhow, it's almost like a habit. I remain aloof and distant because it's safer than showing my vulnerabilities, it's safer than letting people in, because when you do that, when you let love in, inevitably it hurts you at some point. And yet...I also know deep down that this isn't as true as I tell myself it is.

That it's there for me, in people I love. It's in places I didn't think it would ever be again.

PART 2

NON-BINARY LOVE

WHAT COULD NON-BINARY LOVE LOOK LIKE?

Meg-John Barker

For my contribution to this anthology I want to think about what happens if we apply to relationships the same kind of approach that many non-binary trans people apply to gender. Do the binaries that restrict people's gender experiences also restrict our experiences of love? And what kinds of possibilities might open up if we thought and acted in less binary ways in our relationships with others, and with ourselves?

I'll start with a tour through non-binary genders for anyone who is not so familiar with these identities and experiences. Then I'll explore how non-binary ideas and practices might apply to love. Finally, I'll end with one specific example of what non-binary love could look like: the non-binary self-pleasure group that I'm a part of. What does a group of non-binary people jerking off together have to offer us when considering the meaning of love?

Of course, in a brief essay I can only really scratch the surface of what are some pretty huge topics. At the end, I'll point you to some book-length projects I've been involved with which go into much greater depth on all these themes if you're interested.

Non-binary gender

I'm a non-binary person. What does that mean? Non-binary is an umbrella term for all the gender experiences, identities, and experiences that fall outside of the western binary gender system. That's the taken-for-granted cultural idea that people are either male or female: one of two 'opposite sexes'.

In western cultures, non-binary people generally haven't remained in the gender they were assigned at birth because people tend to be assigned male or female. That means that non-binary folks are trans. However, not every non-binary person identifies as trans for various reasons. Also, some prefer terms like NB, enby or genderqueer to non-binary because they'd rather not be defined by what they are not. Others prefer more specific terms or would rather not use a label at all.

The non-binary umbrella

Non-binary is a big umbrella category. Just like the categories of 'man' or 'woman' it encompasses a vast range of different ways of experiencing, identifying and expressing gender. The umbrella includes agender people who don't have a gender, as well as genderfluid people whose gender shifts over time. It includes those who experience themselves as being both male and female, or between male and female on a spectrum, as well as those who regard themselves as being a third gender or beyond that gender binary entirely. Some non-binary people have a very muted sense of gender or find gender completely irrelevant in their lives; others have a strong sense of their gender or would say that gender is hugely important to them.

For me, being non-binary is about embracing multiple sides of myself which are differently gendered. I like the non-binary pronoun 'they' not just for its gender neutrality, but also because it can be used both singularly and plurally. My experience of myself is pretty plural. Being non-binary enables me to embrace more masculine sides of myself that I was encouraged to push down or disown when I was growing up. It's definitely a work in progress. As I learn to understand and embody these different sides of myself the overall 'me' gradually shifts and changes in exciting – and sometimes unpredictable – ways.

Other people's non-binary experience is completely different from mine. Many non-binary folk would say that they were definitely singular – not plural – and would regard their gender as fixed rather than changing over time. Being part of a non-binary group where we discuss our gender experiences in depth every month or so is fascinating. We frequently comment on how helpful it is to have a group where we all share this similarity in experience: the everyday misgendering, the moments of gender dysphoria and/or euphoria, the hugely positive impact when we are actually seen by others. But we're equally struck by the massive diversity in how we experience, identify and express our genders. For some of us it's vital to make bodily changes to bring our outer appearance in line with our inner experience, for others it isn't important, or it's important *not* to make such changes. Some of us want to be read in specific ways by others, others want people to struggle to read us in gendered ways at all. We've all come from different places and are heading in different directions, which give us very different relationships with femininity, masculinity and our non-binary-ness.

These differences also bring other intersections to the fore which matter as much as – or even more than – gender, and which are so interwoven with gender that it would be impossible to disentangle them. We often talk about how our class backgrounds intersect with our genders, for example, or about our various histories in relation to trauma and abuse, or about the widely dispersed geographical locations that we hail from and the different gendered possibilities that were opened up and closed down in our cultures of origin.

The non-binary movement

Non-binary gender is a shifting thing. The non-binary movement or community – or more accurately, collection of movements and communities – is relatively recent in comparison with many sexuality and gender movements. But now it's here it is moving fast.

In places like the UK and US it's fairly new to be able to identify yourself as non-binary, and still not possible on many documents and in many public spaces. Around 1 in 250 people currently identifies as something other than male or female in the UK, when given the chance. But research by Daphna Joel and colleagues[2] has

---

2   Joel, D., Tarrasch, R., Berman, Z., Mukamel, M. and Ziv, E. (2014) 'Queering gender: studying gender identity in "normative" individuals.' *Psychology & Sexuality*, 5(4), 291–321.

found that over a third of people experience themselves as being – to some extent – 'the other gender', 'both genders', or 'neither gender'.

It's hard to imagine what the future holds for non-binary people given that there is currently a strong move to recognise genders beyond the binary at the same time as there's an at least equally strong move to hold tightly onto the binary gender system. Check out, for example, the 71 gender terms offered by Facebook, the issue of the *National Geographic* on the 'gender revolution',[3] the non-binary character and actor on mainstream TV show *Billions*, and the stores which have stopped gendering the toys or clothes they sell. But also check out endless media 'debates' about whether non-binary gender even exists, attacks on charities supporting trans and non-binary people, battles over providing gender neutral toilets, the increasing popularity of 'gender reveal' parties and videos, accusations of abuse against parents who decide not to non-consensually gender their children, and the lack of legal recognition of non-binary genders which remains in most places.

Gender isn't binary

I recently attended a government meeting about this latter issue where we discussed whether it might be possible to change gender policy in my country so that non-binary people could be legally recognised as their correct gender. The way the conversation went reflected the wider cultural assumption that gender is generally binary but perhaps we now have to acknowledge that there are a small number of people who experience their gender in a different way. It's the same 'minority rights' model that has

---

3   (2017) Special issue: Gender Revolution. *National Geographic*, January 2017.

underpinned most LGBT (lesbian, gay, bisexual and transgender) activism.

I wanted to frame the conversation differently and still do. Gender simply isn't binary. We know this from looking back through time and across cultures. The idea of two and only two opposite genders is a relatively new western phenomenon which we – as we tend to do – have imposed on other people globally, often to catastrophic effect, as with the genocide of the indigenous American people now claiming the shared term two spirit. Many cultures worldwide have multiple gender categories, attach different meanings to masculinity, femininity, and other gender expressions than westerners do, and/or regard gender as something that shifts over time rather than something that's fixed in place.

Science is finally catching up with such non-binary understandings, finding that sex/gender isn't binary on any level of biological, psychological or social experience. A diversity of sex chromosome combinations is possible, and there are genes which impact our sex/gender characteristics beyond those on 'the' sex chromosomes. Similarly, the amount of sex-/gender-related hormones that people have, and the appearance of their sex-/gender-related bodily features vary widely. Recent research has found that it's exceedingly rare to have what used to be understood as a 'male brain' or 'female brain' – most of us have a combination of such features. I've used the term 'sex/gender' in this paragraph deliberately, because we're also learning that what were previously thought of as 'biological' sex and 'social' gender are completely intertwined. Our culture and life experiences etch themselves on our bodies and brains at least as much as our body and brain capacities influence how we experience the world.

In spite of this, we tend to stick with rigid, fixed ideas around binary gender. These are bad for everyone, not just for trans and non-binary folks. Shortly before I wrote this essay a BBC TV show, *No More Boys and Girls*, studied gender in the classroom. It didn't even touch on the horrific experiences of gender non-conforming kids (eight in ten are bullied in school, one in ten receiving death threats and over one in four young trans people attempting suicide and nine out of ten thinking about it at some point, according to the Metro *Youth Chances* survey[4]). The programme showed a standard classroom of 7-year-old children, all of whom believed that boys were better than girls, that girls should aspire to be pretty rather than successful, and that girls could only go into professions which were about pleasing others or looking attractive. The boys were generally emotionally illiterate except in relation to anger, buying into all the cultural notions around men's feelings that underpin both toxic masculinity and the high suicide rate among young men.

For me, acknowledging that many people experience gender in non-binary ways is not simply about obtaining rights and recognition for non-binary identified people, it's about dismantling an oppressive binary system that imposes unnecessary norms and expectations on everybody, to the detriment to both their mental health and their experience of work, relationships and pretty much every aspect of life.

Are you with me on the gender binary? I hope you've understood that I'm not saying that we should do away with gender, or that everyone is – or should be – non-binary, or that *you* should

---

4   Metro (2016) *Youth Chances: Integrated Report*. London: Metro. Available at: https://metrocharity.org.uk/sites/default/files/2017-04/National%20Youth%20 Chances%20Intergrated%20Report%202016.pdf.

necessarily question your gender experience. All of these are common misconceptions when discussing these matters. Rather, I'm saying that it would be extremely helpful for all people – non-binary trans folks included – if we could recognise that gender *isn't* binary and loosen the rigid binary rules that currently exist around what the different genders are meant to be like and how they should be treated.

Bending and breaking the binaries of love

So far so good, but what happens if we take this same non-binary thinking we've applied to gender and apply it to love?

That might sound strange at first. Applying it to sexuality makes sense. The division of people into straight or gay mirrors the male/female gender binary. So bi, pan and queer people have similar experiences of invisibility, suspicion and discrimination from 'both sides' as non-binary people.

But love? Do relationships operate on binaries? I believe that they do, and I believe that it can be similarly useful to challenge this binary thinking and the inevitable hierarchies that are inherent in it – the notion that one side of the binary is somehow 'better' or more 'normal' than the other. Here I'll just tease out a few love binaries to show you the kind of thing I'm talking about.

Together/Single
One big cultural binary divides couples from single people and regards the state of coupledom or togetherness as far superior to singledom. We see this all the time in the assumption that single folks must be dating or searching for a partner, and the desperate fear many have of 'ending up alone'. The delights of solo living are

rarely shown in the media, just as the pain, vulnerability and often conflict of living alongside the same person for years and years are seldom emphasised.

As with the gender binary, this binary also obscures all the relationship possibilities that are available between or beyond singledom and coupledom. For example, you might consider solo poly people who have multiple relationships from the place of being an independent unit, and couples who live contentedly apart, or as part of a communal home. Expanding the binary would give people much more scope for finding the relationship with themselves and with others that works best for them, at any given point in time.

Monogamous/Non-monogamous

A relationship binary that I've written about a lot is the monogamy/non-monogamy binary. Again, this tends to privilege the former over the latter, despite non-monogamous relationship styles being far more common globally and the majority of supposedly monogamous relationships in western cultures being – at least at some point – secretly non-monogamous. The rules of monogamous love are so strong that it can be hard indeed for those who try to step outside them to live an openly non-monogamous life. Certainly, there are no legal rights or protections available to those who do so, just a lot of cultural stigma.

Again, this way of thinking also obscures a wide diversity of ways of doing relationships that blur and break the binary. Think about monogamish relationships which are somewhat open, or soft swinging where people have physical or flirtatious encounters with others that stop short of sex. Consider people in couples who stay close with their exes, or who have a rich life of online sex with other people, or who hold a 50-mile rule which enables them to have sexual encounters when they're away from home. Again, moving away from the binary enables people to find a relationship style and structure that works for them.

Romantic/Sexual

Across both monogamous and non-monogamous relationships another binary often remains in place which positions romantic relationships as more valuable than purely sexual ones. It's this approach which privileges polyamory over swinging, for example, and which looks down on 'casual' sex encounters and stigmatises sex workers and their clients. This binary often results in more sex-focused relationships being treated as disposable: ditched by monogamous people when a romantic relationship comes along, or objectified as 'secondary' in non-monogamous communities.

Aromantic and asexual people have usefully challenged the assumption underlying this binary that it's best to get romantic and sexual needs and desires met in the same relationship – and that it's even necessary to have such needs. Many asexual people form close relationships that are not sexual, but which may or may not be romantic; and many aromantic people form close relationships which are not romantic, but which may or may not be sexual. This helps us to start challenging the assumption that our most important relationships are necessarily the romantic/sexual ones, as well as the assumption that we should be getting all these things (romance, sex, closeness etc.) in the same relationship.

Partner/Friend

A final binary to consider on this point is the one which privileges partners over friends. We see that reflected in phrases like 'just friends', 'more than friends' and 'friendzone', all of which suggest that being friends is inferior to being partners. It's this kind of thinking that means we can merrily neglect our friends when embarking on a new relationship and expect to be forgiven for it. Also see how the word 'relationship' in the previous sentence fails to include the very real relationship we have with our friends.

The set of interconnected binaries we've considered here combines to place coupled, monogamous, romantic, sexual, partnered love right at the pinnacle of human experience. Like the gender binary this is quite a new, western thing to do, and is certainly not the way that relationships have been done globally, or across time. The impact is that it puts one love relationship under huge amounts of pressure to fulfil all of our – often contradictory – needs and desires. This often ends up with people leaving each relationship quickly because it can never meet their expectations, resulting in them being bruised by multiple break-ups. On the flip side, it also often results in people remaining stuck in relationships that are bad for them because of the pressure to have a partner, and because challenging any or all of these binaries is so unthinkable.

The self/other binary

Interestingly – perhaps scarily – doing relationships according to these binaries tends to exacerbate another binary: the binary between ourselves and another person – in this case our partner. Black feminist writer bell hooks and others have pointed out that love is simply not possible in a relationship where the self is valued far more highly than the other, or vice versa. What we have under these conditions is the tendency to treat the other person as a thing for our own benefit, and to try to make them what we want them to be. Or we have the tendency to treat ourselves as a thing for somebody else and to try to shape ourselves into their ideal.

All of the following things flow with frightening frequency from the interconnected cultural love binaries I've covered here:

- The privileging of being in a couple over being with ourselves.
- The notion of belonging to someone inherent in many forms of monogamy.
- The assumption that we will let go of our friends and support networks and keep 'the relationship' private from them.
- The expectation that we will squash down many of our needs and desires for the sake of 'the relationship' and perhaps force ourselves to match up to the relationship ideal, for example by having sex of a certain type and frequency even if we don't want it.

It is here that Junot Diaz's concept of decolonial love can be helpful.[5] It situates our current binary ways of loving in our histories of colonialism and slavery, which involved treating other people as things for our own benefit. It imagines other forms of love where we value ourself and others equally. This includes imagining love with consent and care for self and others at its heart, where a critical reflection on power dynamics is ongoing, and where there is a commitment to never treat another person – or yourself – as property that somebody is entitled to in terms of a particular kind of relationship, or form of labour that is expected.

---

5   http://bostonreview.net/books-ideas/paula-ml-moya-decolonial-love-interview-junot-d%C3%ADaz.

The non-binary self-pleasure (NBSP) group

So, to wanking! This is the wonderfully apt-sounding word we Brits use to refer to solo sex or masturbation. Quite a leap, you might think, from decolonising love and dismantling relationship binaries to a bunch of queers wanking in a room together. But this is the space in which I've learned perhaps the most about gender, about sex and about my relationship with other people and with myself.

I should say at the outset that the group I'm about to describe is just one way of doing gender, sex and relationships differently, just one form of love that you might find useful to explore to challenge those pesky binaries. There are many, many others available, the only constraints really being your imagination and the structures and systems of the world around you – which of course clench far tighter around some of us than they do around others.

But I wanted to give you a sense of what non-binary love *can* look like in practice, and I can think of none better – from my experience – than this.

We've been running the NBSP group for a couple of years now. It came out of a mutual desire to form some kind of sexual space in which we wouldn't be continually confronted with the kinds of binary assumptions and misperceptions about gender that many of us were facing in kink or tantra communities, for example. Most of us were still relatively new to embracing and embodying our non-binary identities so it was also a space to discover how they manifested in sexual ways, away from the expectations and existing dynamics of any current sexual relationships. The self-pleasure emphasis meant that we could hopefully free ourselves from being sexual in ways that were designed to please others, and explore what sexual experiences and practices emerged when we focused on ourselves – but with the support and presence of others around us. Of course, one theme that often emerges for us is that even with self-pleasure we're never completely free from the imagined or actual presence of others. But the way we do things at least gives us a degree of separation which enables us to notice this, to reflect on it, and sometimes to shift things.

The group has also ended up being about far more than that. Let me describe for you what we actually do and then I'll reflect on some of what it has taught me about love.

How the NBSP group works
We meet as a group every six weeks or so to spend an afternoon together: from lunchtime to early evening. We've now also introduced a long weekend together once a year. When we started the group we all knew each other, but not very well. Now I tend to see all of the group members one-to-one between our meetings, but so far none of us has had a one-to-one sexual and/or romantic relationship with another member of the group.

We always start our meetings with a kind of check-in session. We make cups of tea and each of us takes ten minutes or so to let everyone know where we're at that day and what's been going on for us since our last time together.

After that one or two of us will lead the others for an hour or so in a practice, discussion, or activity that we want to share. This might be something we've experienced elsewhere, or just a theme that we're keen to explore with others. To give you a sense of the kind of thing involved, over our time together we've tried orgasmic breath practices; we've mapped our genitals with self-touch, words and pictures; we've completed questionnaires to find out about our sexual styles; and we've played Betty Martin's three-minute game to explore our relationships with consent. A couple of sessions which have proved so popular that we return to them regularly are fantasy exploration and 'show and tell'. In the former, everyone has an opportunity to share an erotic fantasy and to talk about what it means to them. In the latter, we each bring something – a photo, object or part of our own body – to show and talk about.

Following the formal activity, we have 45 minutes to an hour of 'freestyle' self-pleasure. For that period, we retreat to mats and cushions in different parts of the room. We're free to interpret self-pleasure in whatever way we want to. Mostly what we do during that time involves some form of self-touch or solo-sex, but it's perfectly acceptable for anyone who isn't feeling it to focus on relaxation, or journaling, or whatever else they feel like doing. As a rule, we don't watch what anybody else is doing because that would be a form of joint sex rather than self-pleasure. But the boundaries are somewhat blurred because, of course, we can all hear each other, glimpse each other and sense each other's presence,

After the freestyle period, we tend to have a short debrief and a small ritual to end that period – perhaps passing around an incense stick or candle. Then we share the food we've all brought with us and chat before heading home. We've all become pretty adept with our vegan, gluten-free culinary skills given that's what's needed to meet all the various dietary requirements in the group. There's often more than one tub of houmous present!

What the NBSP group means to me
It might sound from the description that the important part of the group meetings is the formal activity: the part where new

ideas and practices are introduced which might help us to learn about ourselves. Actually, I would say that all four elements of our meeting are equally important: check-in, activity, freestyle and food-sharing. We've certainly noticed a sense of loss those times when we haven't left quite enough time for one of those aspects – although of course it's also important to be flexible to the needs present on any particular day.

In particular, the check-in has been vital to me. This part of our meeting gets us used to checking in with ourselves before being sexual, which is a vital practice in relation to self-consent and self-care. The check-in allows us to then have a very open and honest consent conversation about how we're going to spend the rest of the time together, given where everybody's at that day, instead of following some kind of regular script. The check-in is also the period where we practise being increasingly vulnerable, thus building intimacy between us: the kind of non-binary love for ourselves and for each other that I'm talking about.

With this sharing there's a very deliberate valuing of ourselves on an equal level with everyone else: both in terms of the time we take up and how we sit alongside each other with whatever's going on and wherever we're at. We've all had times when we've been the most vulnerable one, sharing something exposing or admitting that we're struggling to be present that day. If we're worried that we're taking up too much space, or that we're always the most vulnerable one, then we share that too. We're gradually getting to know which of us tends to occupy certain positions in relation to others, and gently encouraging ourselves to notice that and perhaps to try something different. Nowadays we also often email the group between sessions about what's going on for us, especially when we're feeling particularly vulnerable and in need of support, or particularly proud of something we've managed in relation to our gender, sex or relationships.

Non-binary love in NBSP

How is the group a practice in non-binary love? Well, it certainly troubles all of the love boundaries that we looked at earlier. Self-pleasure in a group challenges the *together/single* binary: are we having solo sex or sex with each other? It's not completely clear.

NBSP also challenges the *monogamy/non-monogamy* binary. Within the group, we have a range of relationship styles from monogamy through polyamory to relationship anarchy. We all find ways to fit the group relationship into those styles of relating.

The *romantic/sexual* binary is also questioned in the NBSP group. We're not having sex with each other, but we're not *not* having sex with each other. It's not a romantic relationship, or is it? As I write about the group now I have feelings of nostalgia, fondness and desire that are pretty close to those I associate with romantic partnerships.

In relation to the *partner/friend* binary, over our time together the NBSP group has become as important to me as any other relationship in my life. It occupies a place among my closest relationships alongside romantic/sexual partners, co-authors, dear friends and companion animals. But a group of people can't be a partner, can they?

I have learned a huge amount from this group about my gender and about my relationship with sex in all its forms. But for me, the even greater learning has been about how I relate with myself and with others. The opportunity to practise being increasingly more vulnerable with people who are not 'a partner' in the standard sense has been a key part of weakening the self-criticism and self-monitoring relationship with myself that has marked my life to this point.

I think we all recognise that the group simply would not work if we valued others over ourselves and engaged in the kind of self-deprecating, self-sacrificing, people-pleasing behaviours that are so familiar to us. We also recognise that it wouldn't work if we valued ourselves over others. So we have to be open about our needs and experiences, and to hearing those of others even when they differ from – or even contradict – our own. For me perhaps the key moments in developing the level of trust that we now have in the group have been when two or more members of the group have conflicted in some way, and have been open with everyone else about that, working through it together with an ethics of mutual valuing, even in their difference.

In relation to those elements of decolonial love that I listed earlier, I think we share a commitment to care and consent with ourselves and others, to continual critical reflection on the power dynamics between us and the relationship patterns we're prone to falling into. We're also committed to treating each other as equal – and different – human beings with respect rather than entitlement, never trying to make anyone be what we want them to be, even when it feels sad or frustrating when they can't offer us what we might like.

I find myself taking what I learn from this group out into all my other relationships in ways that enrich and enliven them on all levels. There is a sense of love expanding outwards, especially when we notice how interconnected we all are within the group, and how this connects us outwards to so many others in our wider non-binary, trans and queer communities and beyond, across the world.

Read more

You can read more about the ideas and research presented in this essay in my book with Alex Iantaffi *How to Understand Your Gender,* and my comic book with Julia Scheele *Queer: A Graphic History.* Alex and I are currently writing a book-length reflection on what happens when we apply non-binary ideas to relationships – and much more – called *Life Isn't Binary* (out in 2019).[6] You can read my thoughts on relationships – including more non-binary possibilities – in *Rewriting the Rules* (the second edition was published in 2018).[7] For more on all of these topics check out my websites www.rewriting-the-rules.com and https://megjohnandjustin.com.

---

6   Barker, M.-J. and Iantaffi, A. (forthcoming, 2019) *Life Isn't Binary.* London: Jessica Kingsley Publishers.

7   Barker, M.-J. (2018) *Rewriting the Rules: An Anti-Self-Help Guide to Love, Sex and Relationships.* London: Routledge.

♡

ON LOVE – GENDERFORK:
A SELECTION OF THOUGHTS
AND FEELINGS ABOUT LOVE

~~~~~~~~

When I first came out as trans there were many resources I used to try and find out more information, and one of the main places I searched was the internet. It was in its infancy back then, but I found many, many useful things on it, some of which were genuinely invaluable.

I read so many blogs, absorbing people's experiences, I frequented message boards and forums wherever I could find them, and I soaked it all up and started to form an idea of who I wanted to be and how I could do that.

There was one site, however, that really changed things for me. That site was called Genderfork, and it's still going today. It was one of the first sites I came across that had photos, profiles and thoughts from people who seemed as if they were coming from the same place as me. It was powerful stuff and it helped me to understand that I wasn't alone and that I could choose how my gender and my identity looked to me, and that that was more than just okay, it was amazing.

For a while I actually volunteered on the site, curating quotes, photos and questions sent to us, and when I was putting this book together I knew I had to feature some of the beautiful, empowering words we received.

Interestingly, although the site itself wasn't specifically looking for things to do with love, a lot of what got sent in was about exactly that. All the quotes in this chapter are anonymous, and all have been published in some shape or form on Genderfork.com.

I hope there's something you relate to here, and I hope you find them as empowering and impactful as I did all those years ago.

* * *

I'm not a woman with facial hair and neckties, and I'm not a man with breasts and a vagina. I'm a little more complex than that, and I wouldn't have it any other way.

I used to really struggle with anorexia, something which came about so unexpectedly that it took me years to get it under control. For a long time I didn't realise how much my discomfort with gender played into it – I hated that I was biologically female, but it was difficult to hide my curves and appear androgynous unless I was underweight. Although I no longer abuse my body and have grown to love myself more, I still have to be wary of old, familiar thought patterns. I find that the more I learn about gender and how I feel about mine, the stronger I become.

I envision a world where who I love and how I dress are not viewed as fringe or something in the minority, something to fear or shun. I want a world where I am embraced as a human being, as an artist, teacher and philosopher. I see a world where I belong.

They're curvy, they're wide, they're plump and make me bump into things. I can't hide them and they make it very obvious of my birth gender when I try to pass. They are my hips and they are the only thing I would never change.

I was looking in the mirror after a shower a few days ago, when I suddenly felt a bubble of happiness rising through me and changing into a big grin: I had realised, for the first time since my haircut, that I'll be able to watch my sideburns turn grey as I grow old.

'*Born in the wrong body*' is not my narrative. I was born in MY body, and every day I fight to love it. I was born in this beautiful trans, fat, ethnic, scarred, flawed body, and every change I make to it and every step I take in it are mine. They are not wrong. I am not wrong. I live and fight and love in this world in MY body.

My dad gave me a tie. I borrowed it for a school trip thing and then forgot to return it. I found it and asked if he wanted it back. He said I could keep it. It's the first tie I wore, the first one I tied. My dad gave me a tie.

My instructor messed up my pronouns in class the other day (I'm trans), but as they spoke they corrected and moved on. No big deal was made, it didn't feel awkward, and I thought little of it afterward. But then I received this email the morning after:

Hi [my name],

I just wanted to let you know that I realise I made a mistake in class yesterday.

I did apologise, correct myself and move on in the lecture but I wanted you to know that I really did feel badly about it.

I hope you can accept my apology. I will try harder in the future to make sure I don't make the same mistake again.

Thank you, [my instructor's name]

There are no words to describe the happiness that I felt while reading that email. I feel truly lucky to have instructors and classmates who respect who I am.

I wish I could sign my name here.

But I don't identify with my ultra binary name and I haven't gotten the courage to change it. If it were up to me I'd just throw caution to the wind and start introducing myself as something more neutral, more comfortable, more me.

I know that I'd end up going by two different names, because my family would never call me something else.

I just came out to my dad, who tends to follow the opinions of my homophobic mom, and I explained to him that gender is a spectrum. Now, I'm terrible at explaining things, but he said that what I told him made perfect sense. Apparently, he had known some gender-defiant kids when he was my age, but he had simply shrugged it off.

When I actually told him about being pansexual, he said, 'Because of how much I respect you, I respect your identity.'

Parenting. Done. Right.

Even though I've felt like I am not a man/woman or male/female for years I've been very good at burying it deeply. In the last couple of years, being around a lot more LGBT people has helped me realise that there are others who experience things similarly and that they feel it as strongly as I do. I'm not alone in that! So, how I see myself isn't crazy even though it often feels as if it doesn't make sense and that has more to do with my culture than me.

A few months ago, I shared with my life partner that I don't identify as a woman or man. Even though it was super awkward and embarrassing for me, he was kind. I was really iffy on whether or not I wanted to use different pronouns and when I decided I did he was enthusiastically ready to make a change. He even discussed it with our roommate, which made it a lot easier on me.

Now that I have someone in my life who is helping me so much in that arena I don't feel nearly so bad about my gender and preference for they pronouns. I'm not ready to talk about all of it but I know that when I am he'll be there for me and it means the world to me. Now, despite moving to a more conservative part of the country I am more secure in my identity.

Yesterday I realised that I'm okay with dating people who are sexually attracted exclusively to members of my birth sex even if I am uncomfortable identifying under it.

I've come so far to know that no matter how their hormones and subconscious see me, the love they have is, in the end, unrelated to my identity and more related to the traits I possess that make me embody that identity and embody my imposed ones. I'm good with that.

I identify as a transgender woman. This year was the first year I was able to go out on Mother's Day as myself. In a daring moment, I participated in a circle of hugs with other moms. It was one of the most emotional moments of my life, a mixture of so many different feelings.

The moment that broke my heart was the moment that I realised that it wasn't what was in my head or in my heart that made you not love me. It was what was between my legs.

Something I'm coming to terms with: My childhood gender conformity does not invalidate my current transgender identity.

I see you. Not the *you* that your parents, your culture or society envisioned. I see the you that you are, and I respect and care for that person. Don't ever give up.

Since I was little, gender had been a kind of issue in my life. Despite being assigned female at birth, I never quite conformed with the expectations.

A moment when I was silenced, which I distinctly remember, was when I was 5 years old, and I came to my mom all upset and told her 'Mom…I feel like a guy.' Not knowing anything about transgender or non-binary people up until this year, my mother affirmed I was a girl and 'always will be'.

Since then though, I had doubted who I was even more. I constantly found myself trying to confirm to people who viewed me as cisgender that I was, only because inside I felt I wasn't.

Up until this year, I had struggled with who I was. Not only did

I find out my sexual and romantic orientations, but my gender identity as well.

I can only say that I'm not male nor female, but I'm also not agender, or genderfluid, and that honestly...I'm just me. What I've come to identify as more accurately is genderqueer/non-binary and I changed my pronouns to they/them. And you know what? I'm comfortable with that. I'd always been comfortable in my own skin, but now it's more than ever.

I'm in the process of coming out (and also getting my hair cut to a length I like better) and I know it's a long way to go, but I've never felt more relieved to know that I was normal, in a way, and not at all tied down to the gender norms or binary that society tried to forcefeed me.

I am a real gender, I don't need to pass and I am completely valid.

PART 3
FAITH AND BELIEF

I don't believe in God, despite coming from a religious background. My family is Christian, and my dad was a vicar. I went to church as a child, attended Sunday school, got baptised and confirmed, and I've read the Bible.

It never really felt as if it was my religion though. I remember when I was 16 my parents gave me the choice to go or not go to church on Sunday, and I immediately jumped at this offer of liberation and told them I don't want to go ever again.

I think that they must have known I'd go with this, but I guess deep down they must also have been disappointed.

I do often wonder if Christianity had been different when I was younger whether I'd be more into it. To me as a young person, though, it seemed so old fashioned and out of touch with who I was. It did nothing for me, it was dull and lifeless, even though I'm sure to a lot of other people it brought much comfort and joy.

And maybe it was a generational thing, maybe that form of worship and belief worked for the generations before mine, but ultimately it didn't for me.

Except, well there was actually a part of it that did work for me. The thing I did get from it was a sense of belonging, just not in a conventional sense.

You see, I wasn't the only young person who had to go to church – there was a little gang of us and we had community. We used to sit at the back, because that's what teenagers do when they're somewhere they don't want to be, and if it wasn't for religion, it's quite probable that we'd have never met and never formed friendships.

Eventually, my family, and myself along with them, moved away from the area. This was also around the time my parents gave me the option to go or not go to church, and so I opted out, partly because Christianity didn't speak to me, but also because my community wasn't there anymore.

When we talk about love, religion isn't always the first thing we think about, but when you really think about it, faith, at its core, is all about love. It's about finding community, or a place to call home, and having a sense of belonging. It's about knowing that you are loved by the people in that community and, for many people, it's about being loved by a higher power as well.

I never really experienced the love you get from believing in God, but I did experience the sense of connection, and ultimately love, you get from a community of people who are like you. Knowing that you're not alone, that someone else gets it, is a truly amazing thing. It's what drives me now to find other trans people. Meeting that deep desire to feel as if you belong, to know you're not alone and to feel loved is essential to surviving life, and even as a non-religious person I can see how having a strong faith must be such a powerful way of achieving this need to connect and belong.

I do sometimes wonder if it would have helped with me coming to terms with my identity as well.

I wonder if having faith, having belief that there's someone out there who genuinely loves you no matter what, would bring any form of comfort, or if having the belief that you're held and loved would be reassuring.

I think it would.

I can see how believing that there's a plan and a reason to everything must help push back against a world that says you don't belong, that you're a mistake. Being able to let that all go must be such a relief.

And of course, as I know myself, faith can give community and a sense of place, or home even, and the love that comes with that. Finding a community that loves you, that doesn't just accept you but actively wants you is so powerful, especially if you consistently feel marginalised and excluded from society.

In so many ways I can see how this must help.

Throughout this anthology, I've been trying to challenge the preconception that love and belonging are unobtainable for trans people, and this is no different when it comes to religion. There's a common misconception that trans people can't have faith, because faiths aren't actually that down with trans people.

And yes, like everything before, there is some truth in this, but it often boils down to the people and the community within that religion rather than the faith itself.

For many trans people, belief fills a hole that they have in their hearts, it gives them community, belonging and love, on both a day-to-day and a spiritual level.

And that is what's important really. As I've said before, we all need love, it's essential to our survival, and maybe belief is a way to get that love. Maybe the answer was with the deities all along.

All of the people who have written pieces for this part of the Anthology are trans/non-binary and all of them have strong belief systems and are accepted by others in their respected faiths.

All of them are pushing back against the stereotypes and misconceptions, and all of them believe.

These are the stories of their lives.

PERFORMING SPIRITS

~~~~~~

Jo Green

I am still very strongly a pagan, but I no longer perform my spirituality. I am in stealth; I don't wear pentagrams or runes or talk to people about my spirituality and how it's changed me. I don't check my tarot reading every time something happens and I don't spend hours poring over the meaning of crystals and herbs. I don't make silly little jokes about how the deities are playing tricks on me or how they're sending me secret messages about things they approve or disapprove of. My spirituality to me is serious business. It's not a lark that people can have fun with. I don't summon any supernatural forces, although I acknowledge them with respect and reverence. I may not perform spirituality but it's something that's within my core and impacts on my day-to-day life in sometimes unexpected ways.

When I'm wandering around and a particular crystal grabs my attention, I take note because I know that my subconscious is trying to tell me something. At Sabbats I may not host or attend any rituals, but I'll take a moment to think about where we are in the season and the general themes that are coming up. I also make sure that I have food or drink that celebrates the season. When I notice the moon, I take a moment to reflect and pay my respects.

I do believe in magick. Magic often features in books, films and shows, whereas magick is the real thing. Magick is thoughts manifesting in reality. At the most basic level, I believe that our subconscious can change the outside world around us. There are two explanations for how it works. Either my subconscious taps into a universal energy, which then enacts change around me, or my subconscious manipulates my behaviour in tiny, unnoticeable ways that then create an impact on the environment I'm in. It doesn't really matter to me which of these is more plausible, the reality is that I have faith that no matter what, everything I'm going through is happening for a reason.

However, this can play out in the weirdest ways. I was at a job where I was desperately unhappy. It had reached the point where every day on my drive to work I would let out a huge scream to vent my frustration, hurt and anger. I wasn't happy about the job I was doing, the people I was working with or the environment I was in. I am also the kind of person who doesn't want to give up and feel as if I've failed. So I created a new situation. I use the term created as shorthand for casting a spell. I didn't do it with all the herbs, incense, coloured clothes and chanting, I created the situation almost without consciously intending to.

In a rather undramatic way, I was fired. It was all very calm and civil, there was no shouting or anything. The boss just called me in and said that they'd 'decided to go in a different direction'. But I'm getting ahead of myself.

It all started when I moved to a new company. It was the first place I'd worked where they had more women in senior positions than men; there was a much more diverse workforce with some visibly queer people working for them, people with tattoos, and people of colour. It started out well. I felt as if this could be the place where I tested the waters, where I tried out being more visibly queer. I started dressing in a more masculine way, leaving behind skirts for men's jeans, and blouses were replaced with jumpers. I increased my dose of testosterone (based on my endocrinologist's recommendation of course), I cut my shoulder length hair short and started generally doing more exercise that would masculinise my shape. When I started down this path, I didn't realise that it's like opening the floodgates.

I'd been ambivalent about my chest for ages. I'd repressed my feelings about my chest, thinking that changing it would not be open to me – until I made the decision that I did in fact want top surgery. What followed was a whirlwind – having a follow-up with my gender specialist, then seeing the surgeon, followed by a bank loan application (which was approved), and getting approval from my manager to take time off work. It was all going swimmingly – until I got my date. As soon as I got the call from the surgeon I started doubting myself. I wasn't sure if I was ready for surgery, what people at work would think, what it would be like. I suddenly started tail spinning. I didn't know if I was making the right decision, but I was too scared to tell anyone.

Outwardly I was fine. I told my manager the dates that I needed to take off work, I started gathering everything I'd need for my recovery time, and stopped watching boxsets so I'd have something to do in my recovery time. I was just generally going ahead and preparing. And then it happened. About three weeks away from surgery I was called in by the boss and given two weeks' notice. Although I'd managed to get a loan for the surgery, it was all based on the assumption that I'd have a job to go back to after three weeks. I cancelled the top surgery (but opted to stay on the waiting list) and started job hunting.

As part of the job hunting process, I changed my style completely. Rather than go back to a feminine performance, I decided to up the scale to more masculine. I got myself a few binders and went into interviews with a more masculine look, in a suit with a button-down shirt. I got a new job and then, on the week that I started there was the greatest snow storm to hit the UK in years. Cornwall, where I would have had to go for my surgery, was completely snowed in and the roads were gridlocked on the day that I would have needed to travel.

This is how my spirituality works. I honestly believe that my subconscious cancelled my top surgery. The possible scenarios are that I was not in the right work situation to be able to emotionally handle top surgery as well as all the abuse and horror of that place. It could have been so that I could move somewhere where I presented as more masculine from the start, thereby removing the anxiety of coming back to work without any breasts and having everyone there gawping at me and talking behind my back. Maybe it was because I needed to understand how much I wanted the surgery by taking the option away to see if I was relieved or disappointed. Maybe it was much simpler than that and it was all cancelled to avoid the snow. I could have had the nightmare of not being able to get to the hospital, or had it cancelled by the hospital, or had it go ahead but be snowed in down in Cornwall, unable to get back home post-surgery. Then there would have been all the issues with having that snow-related nightmare as well as needing to explain to a completely unsympathetic employer why I would need to extend or rearrange my time off (especially because they only had a vague notion of what it was for). These are all really good reasons why, with the best of intentions, my subconscious helped me to avoid disaster.

There is, of course, a part of me that knows that this could all just be coincidence or explained away rationally. But that doesn't matter. At times like these when the world goes to hell, I must believe that it's all for a reason. I must believe that someone is looking out for me and loves me enough to care about how it all falls together (or apart). There needs to be some reason why. And I find it incredibly comforting to think about love on that sort of scale. I don't need the smell of incense, with pentagrams on everything I own. I don't think making jokes about deities forcing you into situations you don't see coming is helpful. I don't need anyone else to acknowledge who I am and how I commune with the forces greater than me. I don't need debates about whether my gender is valid because it's outside the binary constructs of masculine and feminine. But I do need to acknowledge that at any particular moment and in any particular situation I cannot see the bigger picture. I can't possibly know all the forces that are enacting around me that could impact on my situation. For that, I need to have faith. Faith that there is something else out there. Something that makes really shitty situations better. I must have faith that there is something out there much purer than what we humans can make sense of. I must have faith in love.

2018 LOVE

Sabah Choudrey

I love writing. I love water. I love my friends. I love things that keep me going. But I avoid writing about love, I do. I've been trying to write this for a year and it's been difficult. I think about love and my experiences of love and it feels heavy. There isn't a love that doesn't somehow make my heart ache.

Love. Love feels like such a simple word, yet so complicated. Do you know how many words there are for love in Urdu? I don't. But there is not just one. Pyaar. Ishq. Mohabbat. I am not fluent in Urdu but I know this much. One of the first full sentences I learned was, 'main tumse pyaar kartee hoon' (I love you). My mum taught me this when I was a little girl.

There was nothing I loved about Allah when I was a little girl. I was hairy. I was fat. I was...not straight. Not 'normal'. I knew these things. I didn't know much about myself or how the world works, but I knew these things were wrong. It's sad how at such a young age we already know what's 'normal', what's right and wrong. One version of right and wrong, anyway. I heard the phrase, 'this is just the way God made you', and I hated God more and more. I hated myself more and more. Day after day we receive subtle and toxic messages about what it means to be loved. To be loved you have to be important; to be important you have to be beautiful; to be beautiful you have to be silent. That is one version.

How does faith fit into this? When did faith fit into this?

Love isn't something I practise with faith. I think love isn't something that I find easy to associate with faith. Faith hasn't been easy. I think people assume that love is a part of faith and that I love Allah or something, and Islam teaches me to love everyone and everything no matter what. And you stay silent. But I don't. I don't stay silent. I don't love no matter what. Sometimes I don't love Allah. I don't even think about loving Allah because love doesn't make it easy, love doesn't even make sense.

For me, my relationship to Allah is personal. It is understanding, unlearning and letting go. It's understanding that Allah is something so beyond what I've been taught, beyond western Christian notions of a God resembling a person, being vindictive, being a single thing. My relationship to Allah is unlearning these things. And then letting go. I won't understand everything; sometimes I fight with myself to grasp what Allah is and it hurts me, because I can't grasp anything or because I don't know if I believe anything. And that hurts me more.

Do I love being a Muslim? What a question. I get these questions a lot, about being Muslim. There is a default view that no one would choose to be Muslim in this world, especially not if you're queer or transgender, or looking the way you look or behaving the way you do or saying the things you say. There is a default view that there is only one way to be Muslim in this world. There is a default view that being Muslim is a binary. That gender is a binary. That sexuality is a binary. You either are or you aren't. You are one or the other. How many binaries will break my heart? How many binaries does my heart need to break?

Do I love being a Muslim? A question that suggests I would know a life outside my own. I don't think it's as simple as that. I love the relationship I have to faith. I love the journey I have had with Islam, from being raised Muslim, to rejecting Allah completely, and now here reclaiming Islam. I love the questions I still have about Islam, the doubts I have about my faith – this is a part of reclaiming my Islam. I don't love what people hear when I tell them I'm Muslim. I don't love what people see when I 'look' Muslim. I don't love what people say about Muslims, about me. I don't love that I have to think about outing myself as Muslim or staying safe as non-Muslim. I don't love that these are the only two choices most of the time. I don't love what it means to be a Muslim in this world.

Do I love being trans? I think many people assume I don't. The default view is that all trans people hate their bodies, their parts, their appearance, their presence; all trans people hate themselves. We are questioned when we don't. We are talked over when we are not silent. We are applauded when we are proud. We are inspirational porn when we are loved and our experiences are all just tragedies.

Do I love myself? I don't think I do. I don't think I have much room to think about it or even try. I think about who I am – liking certain parts and loving other parts – and all I can think about is the racist and sexist beauty standards I grew up with and how I don't fit into them. I think about the white, skinny, cis-normative body types that I am surrounded by and how I only fit between them. I think about what features I have and how with hormones, makeup and grooming, my gender is read from one to the other to an 'other'. I don't think I have room to think about loving my facial hair, loving my genitals, loving my scars, loving my pigment. People like us don't have room to love ourselves. We're sent messages that we should hate ourselves and to be honest with you, I think the fact that I don't hate myself is enough. It's hard enough to not hate myself, I'm exhausted. It is exhausting. Unlearning those messages of hate, violence, shame, objectification. Unlearning silence.

I think self-love is overrated. Self-love is a challenge. Self-love is a high expectation. Self-love is a privilege, sometimes. To have a safe space and time set aside and resources such as good food, a positive community, inclusive healthcare, access to art, diverse books – these things are privileges.

I think self-like is more realistic.

OUR PLACE

. . . .

Peta Evans

There aren't many places we both feel at home.
This is one of them, and certain nights at the RVT.[8]
FMAS,[9] Wotever, Queer Fayre,
a crowd we fit with – rare enough;
we both like some kinds of museums and galleries
off-season.
But mostly it's this, the tender grumble of the shoreline
on a deserted beach,
picking up pebbles to show to each other, delighted by shapes and tones
and secrets.
Taking the best ones home to add to the garden,
staring at the sea, not speaking much,
letting the waves talk for us.
After five years still tentatively learning each other,
touching our differences in complicated dance,
fascinated by our prejudices taken glorious, desirable skin
(I don't like Americans. You don't like priests.)

---

8   Royal Vauxhall Tavern, one of London's queer pubs.
9   Female Masculinity Appreciation Society, run by Bar Wotever.

so that now you can turn me on in the soft Virginia speech
you learned from your grandmother.
Both of us, in any case, a coil of contradictions to be savoured –
the boy from California who's also my Southern Belle,
the over-academic preacher-man who's also your wee Welsh girl.

There aren't a lot of places we both feel at home.
Not church, that's my thing.
What wounds us, you'll avoid
and I'll approach
with a sort of reforming zeal, but then
you're always a little agnostic about everything,
as I'm always a little bit immersed.
Both of us intensively, extensively
observers, documenters,
using our fingers to smooth in pigments as if onto skin –
caress you with a poem or a picture
to prove I was present
in my own distracted way.

There aren't a lot of places we both feel at home.
It's not as though the world supplies
a world of comfortable space for those like us,
so we're doing pretty well,
we've built a home
mostly of things that others threw away
and we saw beauty in.
As ways of living go,
That's not a bad way
To feel at home.

FINDING HOME

~~~~~~~~

Alex Iantaffi

Falling

I still remember my first spiral dance, a ritual dance central to
Reclaiming witches and often used in ritual to connect and raise
energy. It was utterly unimpressive. It was an unlikely hot day in
July in a park in North London. The baby was fussy, but thankfully
my partner had come along to help with that, the group was small,
and I am not sure anyone had ever actually led a spiral dance
before, as we stumbled over rocks trying to connect with one
another, the green bloods[10] all around us, and maybe raise some
energy. I was going to my first Reclaiming witchcamp the following

---

10 Green bloods are, according to Sami and Reclaiming elder Donald Engstrom-Reese,
all who are part of the botanical realms, such as plants, grasses and trees (http://
wearewalkinginbeauty.org/Walking_in_Beauty/A_Few_Working_Definitions.html).

month and I started to wonder what I had let myself in for. By this point, my expectations were moderate. I had been identifying as a pagan for a few years, reading books, studying assiduously with an online tradition until I realised Wicca wasn't the path for me, self-dedicating myself to this search. Neo-paganism resonated the most deeply in my bones after leaving the Catholic church because I simply could not be myself there. I may still be loved as a queer person but could never know love there. Also, to be quite honest, I had little interest in Catholic churches in northern Europe. They felt cold, unwelcoming and stiff after being brought up in Italy and hanging out with Franciscan nuns and friars and the Focolarini, the movement founded by Chiara Lubich, and the closest experience I had to a mega-church, the closest flirtation with a quasi-cult and a deep sense of home in a religious setting.

I have always had a deep thirst to belong, to be held, loved, embraced and accepted. I have always wanted to find a safe home. Among the few gifts from my father, scattered among the ruins, one that kept me from falling off the precipice of unquestioning belief was a strong serving of suspicion towards any dogma. I came so close to home again and again. And again and again I found that the cost of home might be the suspension of my critical faculties, or the sacrificing of my sexuality, and as for my gender, I was so confused by it that I did not even have any words to describe how I felt besides jokes. I didn't want to be a nun, I wanted to be a priest. *How cute!* I felt as if I was always in drag in my feminine clothes. *How impossible!* I believed in equality and found toxic masculinity suffocating, without having access to the words to describe it at the time. That was maybe the biggest, meanest joke of all that I felt the world was playing on me.

Yet, I kept searching and praying and knowing that somewhere was home. Even though I didn't know what a safe home might look like, I knew that in moments I had experienced a sense of peace, connection and love like no other. These moments would be always in churches, or on peace marches, or demonstrations, or outside with the green bloods, in nature. It was only a matter of time until I would land with Reclaiming, an Earth-based spirituality with strong roots in feminism and social justice. By this point, I knew that neo-paganism was most certainly not a safe home. I had already been told that I couldn't study the runes or be interested in Norse deities because I wasn't 'aryan' as a visibly southern European person living in the UK. I had already slowly distanced myself from Dianic traditions because some part of me knew I needed to reconcile my own inner war fuelled by the patriarchal violence already visited on me if I were to truly find home. And so here I was, on a hot July day, in a park, after reading *The Spiral Dance* by Starhawk[11] a few years earlier, and finding out there was a witchcamp near Glastonbury within driving distance from where I lived. At the precipice, this time, I let myself fall.

In love

My first witchcamp was so different from that first spiral dance! We were working with Bridget and there was a whole team of experienced witches to guide us. I danced and let myself trust and follow my body into the sacred I have always known as home within me. I let the walls fall so I could sense that same sacred flow pulsating in everyone around me and beyond the human circle,

---

11   Starhawk (1999) *The Spiral Dance: A Rebirth of the Ancient Religion of the Great Goddess.* Special 20th Anniversary edition (reissue). San Francisco, CA: HarperSanFrancisco.

with the green bloods and spirit. I dreamed of a spider crawling into my left elbow and knowing I was to be at home with her. I shared my experiences with others and saw them mirrored, helping me believe that this was not some wild fantasy but maybe a way home. I prayed for community and found a teacher who had just moved less than ten miles from my home. By the end of the camp, I had let myself fall in love with the possibility that this tradition could be home. Within months I knew I was on an initiatory path, but I had no idea how far into myself it would lead me. I don't know about you, but when I fall in love my heart expands with each delightful meeting and contracts with each departure. That witchcamp started a long dance with my own healing... This works, I can breathe. I cannot believe they did this, I am choking. Which part of me can be in this dance and which part of me is not welcome? What does it mean to be part of a goddess tradition if you cannot fully love the goddess within you? What does it mean to be part of a goddess tradition if you feel your own femininity is but drag and that there must be more than just horned gods and maternal goddesses? What does it mean to fall in love and not be sure you can be loved back if you show all of yourself?

I had so many questions when I showed up at winter witchcamp a few months later, in another country, on a land I had never met and almost immediately fell in love with, doing magic with people I didn't know but who shared a tradition with me now, a tradition I was exploring. By the end of the five days I was more deeply in love. I was in love with the Reclaiming community in the Upper Mississippi River valley, and with the river itself, with snow, with Freya and the runes, and I started to long for home more than ever. Home had been a longing and it was now an ache in my bones that I couldn't quieten, a song that was guiding me to unexpected desires, a path unfolding like a labyrinth carved out of fresh snow and leading me back to myself. And as many of us do when we are in love, I found myself coming back, again and again. I started to ask myself what would be the cost of not letting myself be whole, if I were truly to be home, instead of wondering what I might need to sacrifice for this gift. I started to understand that maybe I was the sacrifice, the offering making home sacred and possible.

With myself

The initiatory path is rarely, if ever, a straight line, and straight lines have never been my forte anyway. By the end of this specific Reclaiming Feri[12] initiatory path I almost fell off another precipice. The winding roads led me again and again to the brink of facing myself in all my complexity, and trauma and potentiality. I think I fell a few times but there were initiators, teachers, mentors, family, not bound by blood but by love, who had ropes and tips on how to get out of the chasm I fell in. Fall by fall and choice by choice, I found myself at the end of this path that felt like the beginning. I found the voice to claim my gender, not just once but over and over, until I have come to something that feels like an echo of what might be if we lived in a world in which gender expansiveness and queerness had not been nearly destroyed by settler colonialism

---

12 Reclaiming is a pagan tradition whose values are summarised in the Principles of Unity (www.reclaiming.org/about/directions/unity.html). Feri is an initiatory pagan tradition based on the teachings of Victor and Cora Anderson (www.witchvox.com/va/dt_va.html?a=ukgb2&c=trads&id=7737) and one of the influences on Reclaiming. Some people are initiated and initiate others in both Reclaiming and Feri traditions.

and whiteness. Searching for home somewhere, I finally found it within myself. This home was spacious and unknown. In many ways, I am still exploring each room and arranging the furniture. Whereas finding one home in the bi community, after years of identifying as a lesbian, helped me find out that I could be trans and that there was a larger neighbourhood than I had previously imagined, finding a home in the Reclaiming tradition encouraged me to keep searching until I found myself.

The search is ongoing, because how could I ever be done when my home is a breathing, ageing, living system in relation to other systems? However, the ache is not there anymore. Each breath takes me home. Each breath lets me connect. Each breath reminds me I could never be alone. Each breath takes in the same air ancestors breathed. Each breath is a sensuous life-giving kiss with the green bloods. Each breath is a joyous manifestation of life. Each breath is purpose. Each breath is remembrance of all those who refused to fit into the confines of oppression. Each breath is healing. Each breath is learning that this breath is enough. Each breath is dance. Each breath is gratitude. Each breath is love. Each breath is home. Don't get me wrong, this home is not without complications. I have remodelled, because no matter how much I tried to love this home that is me, some things just did not fit quite right. Believe me, I tried. I tried so hard to love myself exactly as I was, and I did. Sometimes love isn't enough though, or maybe it means making choices that are challenging in the short term but give us a little more peace, a tad more ease in the long run. Top surgery was one of these choices. My chest had done its job well, I fed my child, and then I was done. The first time I swam afterwards, it was another coming home, a deeper falling in love with water, my element, and with myself.

In community

I couldn't have found home within myself if I hadn't found home in my spiritual community. Or maybe I could have but it wouldn't have been the same. Since that first stumbling spiral dance on a hot July day, I have found a community more spacious than it initially seemed. My tradition has gone through a process, which lasted several years, to change the one document we are all asked to agree to if we are to call ourselves Reclaiming witches – the Principles of Unity. The document's language was changed to increase inclusivity for people of all genders and gender histories. This process was unfolding during some of the time of my own social and medical transition. To be a part of a spiritual tradition not only willing but resolute to revisit its foundations to ensure they are solid enough for all its members changed me. It's true that I found out more than I wanted to know about some people's deeply ingrained cisgenderism and transphobia. It's true that I also found more allies and fellow travellers than I could have ever dreamed of. I moved thousands of miles to be home with my spiritual community. Home with the river and the lakes and birch, maple and land. Home with my extended heathen queer family, many of whom, but not all, are also part of Reclaiming. Home with myself in community.

This path was also not a straight line, and it was not devoid of macro- and micro-aggressions, of tears of frustration and wails of anger. To be a trans masculine non-binary, queer and disabled Italian immigrant benefiting from settler colonialism by living on Dakota and Anishinaabe land, currently known as Minneapolis, Minnesota, is to be displaced in many ways, which I am still striving to translate into this second language in which I write.

In the midst of all this, there is a missing of home, a connection to the land I was brought up in, where the bones of my ancestors rest, where there is food I can digest because the flour has not been genetically modified yet, where there is language I can relax in as my voice gets louder and more animated. I miss that home yet I couldn't have found home if I hadn't left. I couldn't have found home if I hadn't found the room to breathe and expand. And, because most of the things that have made sense to me I have learned from Black women, I am reminded of Maya Angelou's words about belonging, in a 1973 interview with Bill Moyers,[13] and recently revitalised by Brene Brown for a very different audience. Maya Angelou said to Bill Moyers, 'You are only free when you realise you belong no place – you belong every place – no place at all. The price is high. The reward is great.' I can miss home and know there is no home but here. All these years ago, there was a scent of home at that spiral dance in a North London park. Today, home smells of my children, my partners, my queer family, of winter witchcamp and the Upper Mississippi River valley, of my trans non-binary communities here and across the globe. Today, home smells like me.

---

13   Elliot, J.M. (1989) *Conversations with Maya Angelou (Literary Conversations Series)*. Jackson, MS: University Press of Mississippi.

♡

ON LOVE – THREE LITTLE WORDS (I LOVE YOU)

When did you last say the words 'I love you'?

I said I love you this morning when I left the house on my way to work, like I always do. I'm not saying it out of habit though, I sometimes think there's something wrong with me because I honestly feel this massive wave of emotion when I think about how much I care about her, and that I feel that wave of emotion a lot. Like first thing in the morning, when it's dark and I'm telling her to stay warm and try get some more sleep, and that I love her.

They're no longer for me. My exes never believed them.

My ex said them, a few times. I felt so special.

Last said to Alex before bed last night as I was spooning him

It's been a long time. I doubt I'd believe them if I heard them.

I tell my parents this at the end of a telephone call or conversation, just in case it is the last time we speak to each other.

To my boyfriend, I said it to him after he was ill and we rowed.

I last said them last night, to my chosen brother.

I said 'I love you' to my lover this morning. We have pulled back from a conventional commitment to deciding to choose each other again and again over time and the love feels very present, very joyful, very unburdened and still very grounded.

I said these to my best friend, last night, after a long dinner, before she caught her train home. Since she's moved away to another city, we don't see each other as often, but when we do, it's super intense. She's survived a major, life-changing illness and now every conversation is had on the other side of that – joyously frivolous, intensely refusing to silence or censor ourselves. We've known each other for 20 years, so saying 'I love you' feels like a testament to our survival – of all sorts of violent encounters and also self-harm. It means 'I see you' and 'I believe there is a future' and 'You are connected to this world through me' and 'Get home safely' and 'Fuck sexism/racism/homophobia/transphobia/classism/ableism and all the things that shape our lives, the walls we come up against.'

I said them last night to my partner before we went to sleep. We were cuddling and he fell asleep in my arms and I felt so content.

The last time someone said them was my 2-year-old after he woke up and we snuggled and watched some cartoons before breakfast. His 'ah bu' is the sweetest thing and I can never get enough. My baby is the one person I know that I can absolutely believe when he tells me he loves me.

I said I love you to my granddaughter several hours ago. I feel it's important to be verbal about your feelings on a daily basis. Should never be ashamed to say I love you. And when someone says I love you to me, it makes me feel special and not alone.

Last said to my cat, just now. I was excited to see her. Last texted to one of my partners. In both cases, I felt happy privilege.

I remember like yesterday the last time I said the words 'I love you'. I had finally confessed – come clean – revealed my true self. I told her all about me. No not the man she thought she had married, that most manly of men. No, instead I told her about me. I told her my name, Emily. I told her of my life of torment, how since I was aged 7 I have struggled to suppress my true self. I remember this day like yesterday because I hurt her. I hurt her like I have never hurt her before. I didn't hit her, I didn't strike her, I didn't yell and scream at her. Actually, I never did those things but in that few minutes I hurt her deep in her soul and I destroyed everything. I destroyed her ideal family, her reality of her life, her sense of herself and, worst of all, I destroyed her dreams. I remember well the last time I said 'I love you" because that was the day I lost my soulmate. She stated she was leaving and not coming back. I cried and told her I loved her and tried to explain why I'd never told her who I was – because I was in love and afraid. She stayed for a while but not for me – she stayed for our children. In those few minutes that day, she learned to hate and me – well, I lost my soulmate forever more.

I last said them to my husband. he's sitting beside me. I think he said them first. I felt safe at home. he and I are in a polyam marriage. he had a really good first date last night. I was feeling a tiny pang of insecurity and he reassured me.

PART 4

FAMILY AND FRIENDSHIP

It's fairly safe to say that being trans impacts a lot of my life. Sometimes it's in a positive way, and sometimes it's less so, but nearly always these impacts are in relation to other people.

Part of the problem is that I'm never sure exactly what reaction I'll get when people find out I'm trans. I've written about this in relation to dating earlier, but it also affects other types of relationships as well.

When I came out to my parents, for instance, I genuinely had no idea how they'd react. For a lot of us the first people who show love towards us are parents, and it's often seen as an unconditional love, but there was a part of me that was worried that being trans would be the exception to this rule.

What if the love they felt for me was actually for the person they thought I was before I came out? What if they saw this 'new' (to them anyhow) person as some sort of imposter, stealing their child from them? What if their love for me was conditional?

And once you ask that question then the floodgates open.

When I tell them I'm trans, do I tell them everything? Do I tell them about the pain I've felt for the majority of my life, the steps I've taken to change this, the hormones, the name change, the fact that other people already know and that I didn't come to the first?

How do I know where the limit is? What amount of information is too much information? What is the breaking point for love?

And, of course, it's not just my parents. How many of us have something that we don't express, or don't do as much, or even just don't mention at all, in order to hold on to love?

At what point does doing this become better than no love at all?

It's brutal as well, I know. We're faced with the possibility of living our truth, but losing something that feels fundamental to our existence, or living a half-truth and constantly holding ourselves back to keep something that often isn't even what we really want.

For me, a lot of these fears proved unfounded, but I know that many other trans people are not so lucky. I know people who were kicked out of family homes when they came out, who were cut off in every way from the people that were meant to love them the most, because they dared to live a more authentic life in the gender that was right for them.

That loss is huge and vicious and I don't understand why someone would do this to a child of theirs. As much as I worry about the breaking point for love, it still takes me by surprise when I hear about someone that found out exactly what it is.

However, after a while this theme becomes a part of life. After a while you start to expect that being trans makes love conditional, and that becomes your narrative. I know this because it was my narrative, and sometimes it still is, despite my best efforts.

It's important to say that I don't want this to be my narrative. I don't want to constantly think that any love towards me is conditional on me not being too trans, because actually, nobody is too trans. If the love you receive is taken away as a punishment for wearing a dress or painting your nails, for growing a beard or changing your name, or just not conforming to binary gender roles, then, honestly, that was never love in the first place.

I know it's complicated. I know that when it comes to families everything has the potential to be complicated. I get it. People often talk about the loss they experience when a family member comes out as trans. I've heard people talk about it as if someone has died, and I get why it can feel like that.

There you are, merrily getting on with stuff, when suddenly this person you've known all this time says, 'Actually, you don't know me at all.' You think, 'What? I've put all this time and effort into you being a boy, or a girl, without even thinking about any other possibility. How could you do this to me?'

You think you've lost that person. You think that all that emotional investment counts for nothing now. You think, 'I had no idea. How could I have had any idea?'

The love you've spent time nurturing, sometimes for years and years, was all for someone who doesn't even exist now, except in your memories. How could it not seem like a death?

Except...

There I am, living with this unbearable burden, knowing that I'm living a lie, that I am not the person you believe me to be. Knowing that if I tell you it could mean the end of everything, because I see how much effort you've put into loving who you think I am.

There I am, wanting to let the people who love me the most know about who I really am. But knowing that you'll see it as a death if I do. That you'll act as if I'm someone new, an invader, a parasite, someone who has taken over the person you once knew.

There I am knowing that if I tell you I'm trans you'll love the ghost of who you thought I was more than the real person standing right here – the living, breathing, real-life, always been here, right from the start, person standing right here.

Because ultimately that's the root of it. So you feel grief because your child has come out as trans. I get that it must feel difficult for you, I know that it causes you pain. But honestly, what you're feeling is nothing compared with what every trans person feels.

And that's not to belittle what you're feeling, it's really not. It's just that we need to move forwards with this because it's really starting to fuck us all up.

If you can't deal with your child being trans, or your sibling, or your cousin, or parent, or friend, or complete stranger even (this particularly worries me – why do you even care? Is there literally nothing better for you to do than get upset because some random person *you don't even know* is trans?) then you need to take a look at yourself and ask, what is going on with me? What has changed about this person that I previously loved? Why has them telling me something so personal and so important made me love them less? Why does them being trans matter to me so much that I'd risk damaging that love potentially irreconcilably?

Why has my love suddenly become conditional?

I'm not saying these are easy questions to answer, or that the solutions are going to be clear and obvious, but you owe it to us, and most importantly you owe to it yourself, to ask them.

And just think, if you do ask these questions of yourself, and realise that maybe nothing has changed and that you love them just as much if not a little bit more because they trusted you enough to tell you about being trans, and that ultimately someone being trans should never mean you should love them less than you did before, then just think how amazing your world would be.

The love we have for our friends and family is often messy and confusing. There are a lot of complex emotions involved, which can feel a bit overwhelming. Also, though, this love is often beautiful, bonding and incredibly important to have. We need each other, be that through family groups, friendships or relationships, because when we have each other we don't just make life survivable, we make it remarkable.

The writing in this part of the Anthology is about family, friendships, coming out, and what happens after that. It's about love, both conditional and unconditional, and about how we navigate the path that love takes when family and friends are involved.

These are the stories of how we share our world with the people we love and who love us.

These are the stories of our lives.

TWO THOUSAND AND FIVE

Josie Anderson

I came out to my parents in 2005. It had been a month of coming out, to my partner, to my friends, to her friends, to my work, to too many people.

They were the last people I had to tell, because, honestly, I wasn't sure what they'd say. I was pretty sure they thought I was gay, which incidentally they later confirmed, because I was sensitive and gentle and cried when I felt sad – not what men should be like, as my grandad once said. I know it wasn't meant as a compliment, but to me it felt like one, mainly because I wasn't a man.

I was never a man, it's just that's what everyone thought.

And now I had to tell my parents – my parents who were devout Catholics, my parents who couldn't even grasp the concept of someone being bisexual. Now I had to tell my parents that I was trans.

I remember driving up to Scotland to let them know they no longer had a son, that actually they never had a son, but that they did have something better, a daughter who finally felt safe and able enough to be herself.

Pulling up outside their house I felt scared – how could I not? I knew that other people's parents had rejected them because they were trans, and I genuinely didn't know which way mine would go.

As soon as they saw me they knew that something was wrong, and they started throwing out deathly ailments and tragedies in my direction before I could even start.

In the end I just told them, if only to stop all the guessing.

At first, they were confused, but once I'd explained a little more they were okay. They didn't kick me out, they offered their support, and in that moment, they did everything I hoped they would, they did everything a loving family should do, and I thought it was going to be alright, I really genuinely did.

But then of course the reality began to sink in.

If there was one phrase I heard countless times it was, 'It's going to take time for us to get used to this; you need to understand it's hard for us.'

On the surface it seemed so, well, reasonable. But what it actually meant was that ten years on, we will still use your dead name. We will still misgender you, especially if it's in front of anyone you care about.

What it meant was, we won't tell anyone about you, because we're actually ashamed of you. 'It's nobody else's business,' they say. All I hear is that you're too much for us, why can't you be normal?

'And while we're at it, don't you dare go telling anyone else in the family. It would kill your grandparents,' they say; senicide, of course, being one of the main side effects of being trans.

I stopped telling them things, because although they constantly told me they wanted to know what was going on in my life, and that I could tell them things, what they actually meant was tell us anything as long as it's not about being trans.

'You have to understand it's hard for us,' rings out again and again, a battlecry for the confused and scared.

Because, of course, that's what's really happening.

The love I feel for my parents is strong, but it's also flawed, because I see them as parents. I see them still as how I saw them when I was a child. They were the people I depended on to survive as a child, I saw them as almost godlike, because they provided me with what I needed to live.

As an adult, I forgot that they're no more gods than any other person. I forgot that they're just people. And we all know people. People are messed up. People are flawed, sometimes deeply. People are confused and scared.

And sometimes, it helps me to remember that.

It's getting better. They misgender me less each time they see me. They only occasionally use my old name, and they try not to do it in front of others.

They try to understand what it means to be trans. They tell me how they really liked Nadia from *Big Brother*, and how my gran was defending gay people to her judgemental friend only the other day (I don't tell them that being trans and being gay are kind of different things though, because sometimes you have to take what you can get). They even read a book about Christine Jorgensen who, according to my mother, was very brave and good (again, you take what you can get sometimes).

I'm trying to rearrange the boundaries we have to work better for me. I've taken back control by trying to see them on my terms, when it works for me. If I see them and they say things that hurt me, I try and tell them – not always though, because sometimes it hurts me more to see them looking confused and scared. Sometimes it hurts me too much to see that.

They're not very good with emotions, especially the strong ones I carry with me, but I hope that through gentle and gradual exposure maybe one day they'll manage to be better.

However, I know that maybe this is as good as it will get.

I try not to expect too much from them. I know they can't give me what I really want, not because they don't believe me, or because they don't want to, but because they have never learned how to do things like that. They're both a product of their parents and their ways, in the same way that all of us are.

I love my parents, even though they sometimes do things that hurt me. I try and understand, and I try to let things go, even though sometimes it's really hard. I sometimes wonder if they ever wish I wasn't trans, but I think I know the answer. I also know though that the reason isn't what it was when they were first getting used to the idea of having a new daughter.

The other day my mum shared something I'd written on Facebook that was about being trans. Maybe, finally, who I am is starting to be somebody's business.

ALIAS

. . . .

Sebastian Causton

I'm going to see my parents
And a balance is hard to find
Between which bits of myself I take with me
And which parts I leave behind.
They have issues with my queerness,
But for the first time they are trying to try,
And this has got me thinking that maybe so should I.
I guess I could wear a hat to shield them from my shaved head
I guess I could swap my boxers for lady pants instead.
I guess for just one weekend I could manage not to bind
And instead of being an angry queer, I could pretend that I don't mind.
I guess to make my Dad smile I could wear a dress
And act like everything is fine and I am not a mess.
I guess I could put mascara around my eyes,
A small mask to hide behind, just adding to the lies.
I'll let them call me daughter
And I'll let them call me she
Even though every word is like a bullet to me.
I could pretend that I am ok,

Be gracious and smile,
Avoid topics like work have suggested I get signed off for a while.
I can't talk about my friends,
Because most of them are queer,
Or if they're not they understand a queer life is happening right here.
I can't talk about my job because I work in sexual health,
And they see sex as something that revolves around a queer self.
I can't talk about where I live because Brighton is 'too gay'
And living here has affected me in a detrimental way.
I can't talk about romance, but I've had six years of that.
I keep the fluttering of my heart silent, I've got it down pat.
I can't say what I'm scared of because it would frighten the fuck out of
them too
I can't say I'm worried I'm drifting from you.
If I leave all this behind, then what have I got left?
I'd be empty, nothing, bereft.
So I know you are trying, and I want to too
But if I don't bring all of this
I can't give myself to you.

TONES OF THE CAPARAZÓN, OR THE LIZARD BRAIN'S RESPONSE TO MISGENDERING BY FOLKS WHO SHOULD KNOW BETTER

Ariel Estrella

When I'm home, and my brother is home, and the evening cracks our hearts open just so, he and I have kitchen talks.

I check in with how his day was every time I see him, but we don't always kitchen talk. We can't, not with the way we go about it. We will camp out for hours in our narrow kitchen, exhausting ourselves as we chat and snack from the fridge and the tray of goodies stacked on top of the microwave.

Usually we marvel at how weirdly parallel our lives always seem to be. Once, though, we end up on the topic of friendzoning.

I see him wanting to defend the straw man nice guy who feels betrayed by a girl friend who won't be his girlfriend. My brother talks in half-steps, never settling down on an opinion, but clearly remembering his high school not-sweetheart or perhaps some upvoted Reddit post he read the night before.

In the vulnerable space we build with the stove as our witness, we yield easily to each other's wisdom, so much so that we never find need to interrupt one another. But I come close to speaking over my brother that night with how hard I spit my words as he pauses for a breath.

I tell him that I get it. I do. I get how much it sucks to like/love/lust a friend when the friend does not feel the same back. I get the whirlwind of emotions that accompany crushes and infatuations, and how sometimes it feels like the strength of my emotions alone should entitle me to requited love. But I also remember the boy in senior year who hugged me sweet every time he saw me...until the day I rejected his offer to hook up. He hadn't yelled but his eyes grew sharp. Angry. I never heard from him again.

To have someone – to have a man – angry at me because I somehow did not fulfil his expectations is frightening. It makes it hard to trust men who seek me out for friendship.

My brother asks me, offhandedly, for what a woman feels when a man who's a stranger approaches her, even if it is obviously an offer of friendship. I don't say I am not actually a woman; I think to but I don't because even here in our kitchen my gender feels too big and aching to tell him. Instead, I confess the first thing that comes to mind: *I can't speak for women, but...for myself, when that stranger comes, I am imagining just how many ways a man can hurt me.*

* * *

I never felt anger, or so I had said. It wasn't that I wasn't an angry person, but that I either had forgotten how to feel the emotion, or had chosen not to so hard that my discipline alone carried out my wish.

I felt proud of the absence of anger in my life. I was superior, better, more stable – but in comparison to who?

The straw man, of course. The stranger men, and the familiar men who I've cared for and who hurt me, and all the people who have scared and offended me and made me feel vulnerable.

I could not be an angry person because I refused to be a violent person. There hadn't been a difference between the two. I was not a violent person so I couldn't be an angry person because anger meant punched walls, red faces, fists and slaps thrown, hair yanked by its ponytail, and objects broken under rubber wheels.

I was not angry, because I was not violent. I couldn't be angry. I wouldn't be angry, because I wouldn't be violent. I would be loving and forgiving and generous instead.

Or so I had said.

* * *

When I started working, I wasn't out as non-binary.

I knew before I interviewed at one of my first employers that they weren't set up for trans inclusivity, but that wasn't enough to scare me away from the organisation. They were an amazing non-profit set-up, I loved my colleagues like cousins, and I thought I could help them confront their cis-normativity. I believed I could use my position of power as a staff person to support any trans people we served or would serve once our programmes could more tenderly hold our identities in the world. I would never have to bring up my identity if I angled to effect change gradually in the organisation, without it taking place through me.

Then, during a staff meeting, leadership decided to make inclusion of pronouns into our email signatures mandatory.

Mandatory pronouns in signatures was a great attempt at promoting trans inclusivity. However, while they are meant to challenge cis people into being more trans inclusive, mandatory pronouns can also negatively impact any trans people who want to choose when they do and don't come out.

Case in point: me.

I could make some compromises in my choice to not be out, but I could not put she/her/hers in my signature to maintain my privacy because I refused to misgender myself in my every email interaction. Making the inclusion optional at least gives trans people the agency to do right by themselves. But even if it was made optional, I'd been so vocal about how the organisation needed to be better about LGBTQ issues. I worried that people would question me or my signature should I forego inclusion, and I didn't want to come up with a lie for why I didn't include my pronouns.

I was ~~not angry, not angry, not angry...don't be angry, can't be angry, can't be. I was just...~~disappointed by my colleagues for forcing my hand. But I decided to be generous. I decided to understand that my colleagues could not have anticipated that this was the last straw for me. It did prove, however, that the organisation had work to do for trans inclusivity.

* * *

So, I convinced leadership to make pronouns optional. I put

they/them/theirs into my signature, and I came out. I didn't want to. But I did.

And then, the misgendering started.

* * *

I expect violence.

When people are angry or tense or frustrated or insensitive in response to something I've done, no matter how much I care or love them, no matter how much I am in the right, I shut down; I remain still; I go quiet. And it's not really their anger or tension or frustration or insensitivity that frightens me, but the potential of violence I imagine within it.

My flinches are as much trained into me as the drool of Pavlov's dog's hungry maw. In some primal lizard part of my amygdala, I do not frame intimate friendships and relationships as just that; this lizard brain, once spurned, redefines intimacy. Getting close to a friend or partner now also means opening myself up for more risks, more opportunities for greater violence and harm. There is no one who can be the one who 'would never do something like that!' We – the reptile and I – have learned that current safety does not guarantee future safety. Instead, safety can only be defined relative to the violence and peace I've known in equal measure.

I don't care about strangers misgendering me. Given my body type, it's extremely difficult for me to be legible as genderdifferent, and I am too anxious, resource-strapped and lazy to engage the politics of passing beyond a shrug and 'better luck next time'. I fear strangers because I fear most human interaction, but I don't really care about them and their assumptions about my gender.

But when I'm misgendered by someone who should know better, by someone I care about, I freeze up. I tense up. I breathe in.

I breathe out. I hope they notice my pain. I hope they will correct themselves. When they don't, I wish to correct them. I want to correct them. I think about if correcting them will make them angry. I don't want to make them angry. I can't make them angry at me. I swallow around the reptilian fear that corrupts the trust I have in my peers. I can't say anything, so I say nothing. I give myself a moment to calm down my fear. Then I move on.

I hope the person will remember my pronouns next time.

* * *

I wanted my colleagues to switch right away, but they didn't. They didn't, even though the one thing I asked for was that if they couldn't use they/them/theirs automatically, they at least needed to correct themselves. I wasn't expecting perfection, just correction.

It hurt so badly that the possibility for people to use my pronouns was out there, but no one respected me enough to refer to me correctly or to catch themselves when they messed up. ~~I was so angry, no not angry, never angry, can't be, no not~~ I understood that some grace was needed. I gave them my patience.

Some time passed and nothing had changed and still hardly anyone corrected themselves. I sent out emails, individually and staff-wide. I humiliated myself explaining my physical responses in detail, so people could understand how to notice my offence when I'd been misgendered. I even joined a women and non-binary non-profit professionals workshop series, and I centred my learning on how to be out at work and how to not freeze up so I could react to misgendering in a more constructive way.

At first, I thought it was getting better because I heard the misgendering less. Unfortunately, I realised that the only reason I was hearing it less was because I was physically out of the office so much thanks to a series of offsite events. Once I settled back into my cubicle, I was misgendered at least once a day – at the very least – and almost entirely without correction. Worse, I knew that that was just what I overheard, never mind what must have been going on when I wasn't in earshot.

I made so many concessions, and for what?

* * *

There's a conflation that inevitably happens by allowing two things room beside one another. Here, in this essay, I speak around the very intense physical violence I experienced from people I loved and who loved me, and I do so in the same precious few pages as I discuss misgendering in an office setting.

To fit these two pieces together is to wrestle over their disjuncture – I worry that the comparison is inappropriate. I worry that I sound like an idiot pouring disparate tensions together and expecting the two parts to stick. For vinegar, I build echoes of that poor hungry bruised kid I once was, even as I skirt around the true depth of my trauma with pretty gestures of purple prose. For oil, there's me, older and college-educated, whining about my cushy job even as I enjoyed the privileged cradle given to white collar millennials participating in the non-profit industrial complex.

Most days, my worries win out. On these days, I quickly sweep aside the raw and vulnerable place that being misgendered puts me in. I shouldn't have to, but I do. I do because I may expect violence, but when I am actually harmed again, my first impulse is to dismiss the new thing as not bad enough. After all, I have lived through worse: I can manage any pain or unpleasantness because I survived hell; I can accommodate a little disrespect as long as it's not a purpling bicep – nothing could be enough to warrant my anger, frustration, or hurt.

But then there are moments when I see the situation clearly for all that it is. Moments when little stresses and little offences balloon into huge disruptions to my life, because I've just been misgendered by a friend who should know better and I'm too busy coping with that to handle the new thing coming my way. I sit at my desk for hours feeling displaced from the beautiful, calm space I have carved for myself at an organisation filled with people who are dear to me. I produce less. I feel like a failure as a worker and as someone proud of themselves and as someone who cherishes all of who they are.

It's during these moments that I allow myself grace and I remember: misgendering is not my fault. It's not me being sensitive. It's not me overreacting or not being patient enough. It's not me burdening my colleagues when I ask them to use my pronouns.

Colleagues misgendering me is inappropriate, unprofessional and disrespectful. It interrupts my work. It upsets me greatly. It takes time I could be doing a million other things when I have to correct people and/or cope with the misgendering. It is a hostile act against me that I feel shamed into forgiving because it appears to be so small and innocently ignorant. The responsibility of always correcting people when I am the one being misgendered is taxing, draining, unfair, and yet expected of me. Colleagues misgendering me is not okay.

Loved ones misgendering me, however, is its own kind of heartbreak.

* * *

I burst.

* * *

Date: Wed, July 13 at 6:48pm – 0400
Subject: Complaint regarding our organisation's compromised transgender inclusivity [Excerpt]
To: 'Executive Director', 'Development Director', 'Program Director'

Dear senior staff,
Misgendering me is extremely pervasive and seems so easy for the staff to do. I am writing to you as senior staff to say that we as an organisation need to find constructive and concrete ways to stop it.

I am currently unable to defend myself against the disrespect of my colleagues, other than the rare email when I am confronted with the unsustainability of dealing with misgendering in silence. That does not mean, however, that I deserve to continue to be disrespected.

We as an organisation can work at the institutional stuff over time. We as an organisation can figure out ways to ensure we are more transgender inclusive in our projects. Real change takes time, and I get that.

But something needs to change. Soon. Because I shouldn't have to wait to be respected by my peers.

There needs to be some urgency to make sure that from day to day, I'm respected and treated with the dignity I deserve. When I decided to come out, I wanted to make change at this organisation for the better so this kind of nonsense didn't happen again. This is, once again, an attempt to offer my resources, time, patience and generosity so that we as an organisation can do better.

We need to do better, if only just to keep true to our mission that we all got engraved on our tongues.

* * *

I got one immediate response to my email: a kind apology from the programme director and an offer to have lunch to discuss things. I followed up to arrange a time. I got no further responses from him.

Six days passed without a single additional comment, even though the organisation's employee handbook states that complaints sent to the executive director must be responded to within a week. Furious and hurt at being ignored, I sent a snippy email to the director with a reminder saying that I deserved a response, if even just a read receipt.

Only then did I get one. Without a comment directed to the reasons for my distress, the director tore into me about my unprofessionalism and (an accusation I will never forget) my hectoring tone.

* * *

Talks with my ma are not bound to the kitchen, like they are with my brother.

We sit together on the train, on our way to a fancy dinner with my girlfriend. The muted orange of our plastic seats filters the conversation with an edge of nostalgia. I tell my mother I am writing an essay on anger, or something like it, for an anthology about love. The connection doesn't surprise her, nor does the fact that it would be a topic that interests me. She's known anger and love and anger in love, and knows I know it too.

I ask her: *How was I then, when everything was going on?*

She doesn't answer right away, and I lean into her shoulder to wait out the silence, although it's not long before I start to anticipate her response. I expect a mention of our phone calls, when she said she wanted to jump off a bridge knowing I wouldn't leave my unsafe situation and I in turn called her a bitch and told her I hated her, just because I felt cruel. I expect a mention of when I finally moved back in with her – those terrible, awful, furious months I snapped at everyone and cried all the time. Or a mention of how spitefully I attended classes when I bothered to show up, when I would whip out my laptop and omegel with strangers in full view of my teachers to show them I didn't care.

'*I don't think you were actually angry,*' my ma says instead. '*Just indifferent and hard. Like you had un* ***.' She's speaking in mostly Spanish which I can usually follow, but this is a word I don't know. I don't even know how to spell it. She tsks, '*You know,* ***. *One of the lizards has it. Como...como una tortuga.*' I use the underground MTA wifi and it takes a moment to google, but together we suss out the word: un *caparazón*. A shell. '*You built up your caparazón to not let too many things hurt you. It was necessary for all the changes we lived through. We weren't in a settled or quiet environment. So I had it too: a very strong, very hard heart.*'

Subway platforms blur past us beyond the train's jaundiced, scratched window as the hand at her chest flexes into a claw. Curled up into her side, I can follow the pull of every wrinkle at her knuckles. *For all that I lived through, I couldn't even think of not moving. Some people stay in their happy place. Their family stays in the* same place, in the house their grandfather lived, and their father lived, and they live. And they are happy – but nothing happens.

We were always moving. We look for a thicker shell.

* * *

When I first came out as trans at the organisation, I ended the announcement email to my supervisor with a personal note: *To you specifically, I wrote, I want to just say thank you for your support for all these years. Even if I was not ready to be trans here, it still meant so much to me to have you as a mentor. I acknowledge that this news might shake things up personally for you, if only because it shifts something fundamental you assumed about me for so long. I just hope my choice to do this through email isn't read as me thinking any of this is impersonal: I feel brave through my writing, the kind of brave I haven't been able to be outside text on a screen with regards to my trans identity.*

It's obvious to me now how carefully I approached her feelings, even though she was one of the ones who made me feel that the space could not fully support me as a trans person. My coming out was from a reactionary place, not from one where I was centred as an empowered agent with total control over how and when I disclosed my identity and pronouns – and it shows.

Still, I wouldn't change my email or the grace I shared with her. Because when I find relative safety, I hold onto it with jealousy.

I found relative safety at this organisation. When it was good, it was truly wonderful. I had positive interactions with the organisation even before I was hired as staff. Then when I joined the team, I believed in their mission and the network of beautiful, thoughtful, creative people I found there. I knew we made real change in the communities we served. I fell in love with the community around me, and I cherished the space I found for myself.

I loved my colleagues. Well...okay, the executive director was actually kind of an asshole who I didn't like that much. But, everyone else I loved. I adored each and every one of them, and I knew they adored me.

Even as they misgendered me, I loved them. Even as they misgendered me, I couldn't just tell them to fuck off. I wish, sometimes, I could drop people in an instant if they dare harm me. If I heard this story from someone else, I would be tempted to say that those folks aren't really their folks if they are misgendering them so severely. But, I know in my heart that when I worked with them, the people in the organisation were a beloved community to me. And as such, I decided they deserved to receive my hard-earned but freely given patience.

Often, this patience is really just the shell my mother named. My shell is how I shore up armour around myself; only with time can I break through it to acknowledge the pain I feel underneath.

Yet, I have learned that I am made brave and loving at my own pace, slow though this pace may be at times. With patience, I can hold my fears with the reverence they deserve. I can settle into how my struggles define me, make me strong, made me see the beauty of the world in my own distinct yet treasured way. I can manage my PTSD. I can see the ways to name my frustration while always allowing the potential for growth. (*I am always moving, changing, looking for a thicker shell.*)

Because of the time it takes me to get to this resilient core, I can find what I so often deny myself: an anger without the threat of violence. It's a righteous fury, but it's an anger that never forgets my generosity and the care I feel for those around me. Instead,

I can craft a framework of restorative justice, where the person harmed and the person who has harmed can find peace with one another again.

I want to be better at immediate and in-person reactions. I want to recognise my anger as it happens and not have to suffer until I reach a breaking point. I need to respond to my unhappiness quicker.

But for now, I can at least allow myself the grace of a moment to process before I act, just as I would for any of my friends. Because even as I flinch and worry and hold myself back from the fullness of my fury, I have learned one thing over the years: I love all that I am, lizard brain and all. And with this love, I forge new paths where I effect change fully myself so my community not only has good intentions with our work, but a good impact and good results as well.

* * *

With gritted teeth, I arranged a meeting with the executive director to discuss my complaint. While tense, everything actually turned out pretty okay. The director admitted I was right, we set up procedures to better address the issue, and we called in an LGBTQ sensitivity workshop facilitator. It took another three months until the misgendering stopped – and even then it was mostly because of staff turnover and the new people didn't know to call me by anything other than they/them/theirs. Still, a success nonetheless.

MTF, SEEKS LOVE, MAYBE MORE

Emily

I love love. I love that love is a 'doing' word and a 'being' word. And a 'having' word. For me, love has been something very consistent and affirming – even when I doubt everything else about me, I always know that I still love love. And being a trans woman certainly intersects with how I relate to love. But not exactly in the ways that you might expect.

For me, a lot of being a trans woman is anxiety. Lots and lots of anxiety. Am I 'passing'? Am I safe here? Will this person yell at me? Did that person see me as male or female? Basically, a lot of these thoughts relate to the external, to what other people are thinking. And I think this anxiety about what random people might be thinking also bleeds somewhat into my private life. Actually, I am pretty worried about what other people are thinking a lot of the time. Even my own self-worth sometimes ends up bound up in what other people are thinking in their own private worlds.

But love is an escape, and more. In a moment of experiencing love, it's as if the walls between our internal monologues have broken down – each kiss, touch, gesture and 'I love you' is like a window into another person. We are just our souls existing, pressed up against one another and feeling the most wonderful freedom and excitement. And there is not just one type of love. In fact, I'd go as far as to say that if every love is unique, there are infinite ways to love and be loved. Romantic friendships, random sexual encounters, phone calls with a lover half-way around the world, watching TV with your soulmate. Those are just some examples. But deep down we all know a love when we feel it.

I love that being trans and queer has let me take a step back from what society has decided is love. I feel as if I've been allowed to see that love is a big house, with many rooms. Love is not limiting or limited. I love people, and when people love me back. Well that's just lovely.

HIDING FROM THE WORLD

～～～

Freiya Benson

You pull your hood up around your head, and your softly contoured face falls into shadow, obscured by the cloth. You tell me that you're cold, but I know why you hide your face from the world.

I know that you're just readying yourself, battening down the hatches, preparing for the oncoming storm.

You pull your jacket on, over the grey and black hoodie. Another layer of protection, another piece of safe, to hide you from the looks all of us are too used to now.

Sometimes we talk about standing out. Sometimes you tell me that we're witches, strong, powerful, untouchable. We stand out because we're not like other people, we straddle worlds, boundaries, preconceptions. We are witches, but we are also so much more.

When we are mighty, nothing can touch us, but sometimes that might comes at a high cost. It's hard to maintain strength when every look can have the power to knock you down. It's hard to stand tall when you're attacked by people who don't even realise they're doing it, because their worlds are smaller than yours.

You tell me you want to shout in their faces, to tell them to fuck off, to push them away. You tell me how they call you 'mate', how they use pronouns that are not yours, and I feel for you. I know that pain so well, it's been a dark companion of mine for longer than I can remember, and now it's leeched itself onto you, whispering in your ear, corrupting both our worlds.

I want to hide from all this, I want to shut it away, to make it stop. I see that in your face when I look at you sometimes, your hood pulled up tight, shutting out the harsh realms, pushing the dark companion from your ear.

But when I see you reflected in me I also see the other side.

I see the fire. God, that fire. I can almost hear it crackling behind your eyes. It's in your voice when you tell me how you look up and catch the staring eyes, when you correct the words that don't fit your gender.

And I nod, and I agree, and I feel that fire in me. God, that fire. That fire is what makes us witches, that fire is what makes us mighty and unstoppable. We are the fire of change, burning bright with our words, our actions, our existence.

We don't need the protection of clothes, the safety of non-existence, the invisibility of blending in, not when this fire runs through us, coursing like a raging torrent. Pain, anger, pride, love – emotions we all know so well, like old friends, as strong as the person who carries them, as mighty as the people we surround ourselves with.

That collective fire, that fire, it never burns us, even though it can burn others. They try their best to put it out, with their words, their actions. They aim for the source, because they're experienced at this and they know what tools to use: a wrong pronoun here, a denial of identity there. They try their best to put our fire out, but they don't know the thing we know.

They don't know that every flame they crush, every life they extinguish, every person they hurt with thoughtless cruelty and blind prejudice, makes our fires burn brighter.

They don't know that every trans person murdered is another reason for us to fight harder. They don't see that every act of violence makes that fire more consuming, more urgent, more of an unstoppable force.

Their hate feeds the flames of change. We are that change, and that change will come because of us. They are just the catalyst, the fuel, the reason.

Every time I want to hide, to pull my hood up over my head and just have a break, I think of these words.

Every time you hunch your shoulders and steady yourself for the storm, I want to lean in and whisper over the dark companion on your shoulder. I want to whisper and tell you how we are living fire, how it is coming out of us, breath after breath, till it drowns out the darkness, like fiery stars, blazing in the skies, turning night into day, letting everyone see what we already know.

We are witches. Mighty, unstoppable, beautiful and unflinching. Just try and stop us.

Just you fucking try.

NON-FICTION

Max Guttman

I stopped mid-conversation and jumped over a chair to say I liked your shirt – Calvin and Hobbes flying a TARDIS sled past Dalek snowmen didn't care that the blue purple orange print didn't match the green cotton they're my nightmare antidotes after playing Aaron and Coach Carr in *Mean Girls* we watched *Bridge to Terabithia* on my bed and pulled our sweaters over our heads when he went to the art museum and still cried even though we've known the story since middle school late night in the library I pretended I was reading *Orlando* while you scrolled through Tumblr and we laughed too loudly at dubbed cats drank fake hot chocolate at Tea Garden and snapchatted pictures of fruit to your friends who kept saying date date date and imagined what it's like to be famous showed you *The Perks of Being a Wallflower* and we giggled when Sam had an English accent and you first took my hand when Charlie realised his Aunt Helen's touch hadn't always been good it was one-thirty you were tired from tears and I said you could stay that first night I had a bad dream but you were still there snoring a little bit and I left my klonopin on the nightstand we bussed to the art crawl almost walked into someone's apartment thinking it was a gallery with an Invader Zim door and talked to a grandmother who mixes glass beads into paint so her canvases glitter decided to make ourselves official so we added it to our timelines and watched the reviews stream in sitting in the park next to F. Scott Fitzgerald and the birds that kept flying up and around and down and reminded us of Alfred Hitchcock and our years in school marching bands playing music from *Psycho* and *Batman* ate a rushed dinner over cafe plastic flowers so we could make it to *The Cradle Will Rock* on time and you laughed yourself to tears when the boy who says sir and ma'am offstage motorboated the air Pokémon battles over wifi five of us sitting on the floor until batteries died so it became storytime but when the topic turned to exes you nudged me and we left and you said you didn't want to talk about it Tumblr on my couch Photoshop edits and lipsyncs and cartoon gifs and you tickled me until I fell off onto the wood floor it was loud but didn't hurt my roommate said no being gross on the couch and grinned I started crying in my sleep blood from blistered memory and you pulled me against your chest and told me it was just a dream this time he wasn't here you were first snow southerner claimed you'd snowball like Buddy the Elf left our backpacks in the field so we could run faster and gather ammo and threw and dodged and said we were accidentally in each other's line of fire we were going to go dress shopping change up your wardrobe for the ball like Cinderella but you said you weren't feeling confident enough to go out I didn't hear from you for two days after that library carnival blow-up horses bounce through the bookshelves fabulous photobooth shoot in the study room dance in front of the printers last hurrah before finals on the couch writing your nanowrimo my comic book you so silent you started to cry said your first your friend your first morethanfriend his touch hadn't always been good your blisters too raw you thought they were callused still rub can't see me without seeing him can't do this anymore you said need to be friends best friends pinky promise put out my little finger forced my voice steady never dream of making you feel guilty for what he did to you and I knew the story too one day it'll be a story a timeline point a ten-week tale but once upon a time it was real.

THE RENTS

. . . .

Silver

I want to write about my parents,
but it's hard
because what I want to say isn't always kind
and it isn't always good.
I want to say to them
you know you messed up right?
I want to say to them
when you use my old name, my old pronouns
that it cuts me like a knife.
I want to shout at them
it is so easy
it's just a few words you need to change
you do it all the fucking time with everything else
you even correct people when they call your dog he
so why can't you do it with me?
I want to ask them why
why is my chosen name so hard for you to say?
why don't you give enough of a shit about me to use she?
why do you say you love me

and want to see me
and know how my life is
then push me away
with your sharp hard words?
That's what I want to say.
God fucking damn it.

So anyhow, I have therapy.

Because I know that if I say these things
they'll say
we didn't know
you never said
you played with cars
you liked the colour blue
you were our boy, and we can't let go of that right now.

TEXTING BACK 'I LOVE YOU TOO'

Faith DaBrooke

Planning a going away party, or a party for some other significant occasion, and having no one show up has always been a great fear of mine. My sixth birthday party at the roller-skating rink happened to coincide with a major storm. As a result of the weather, no one showed up, leaving me as devastated as a brand new 6-year-old can be. So when Sarah, a not quite close friend on the periphery of my social circle (she was in fact a member of my brother-in-law's Dungeons & Dragons group), announced a going away party, I figured I had to go. You don't want even a tangential friend left alone on their last hurrah in Brooklyn before they move down to Atlanta.

It was good that my partner and I went to Sarah's going away party, for more reasons than one. When we got to Royal Palms shuffleboard bar Sarah was all by herself. It was simply her, a hundred empty booths, a gleaming shuffleboard, a few scattered board games, and a long bar that featured advertisements for fruit-filled tiki drink specials. With drinks in hand we talked with Sarah of her future endeavours down south in the land of a thousand strip malls, all the while feeling a little bad that we, mere tangential friends, were the only ones who had showed up to bid her goodbye. Our pity would abate when another friend of hers, Jessica, arrived.

At this point in my life I was not yet officially transgender. Yes, I've been transgender and had gender dysphoria for my entire life, but I had not yet decided if transition was right for me. Nevertheless, I took almost every opportunity I could to present as female. Say, opportunities like a tangential friend's going away party. As it was summer I wore a new sundress I'd picked up, along with sandals to show off my pedicure. And to new people like Jessica, I introduced myself as Faith and used all those good female pronouns.

Soon after her arrival we all headed over to a nearby barbeque joint to get food. All four of us grabbed a booth and the waiter referred to us with that most wonderful of words: ladies. He was tall and lanky with a goatee and a ponytail. Together, we four ladies concocted an elaborate picture of his basement-dwelling life. We imagined his wall of samurai swords, the two or three magic tricks he used to try and impress girls, and of course he had a pet snake, that almost went without mentioning. Okay, it's a little mean, but we did tip well.

After that I am not quite sure how Jessica and I became friends. We had exchanged numbers and friended each other on Facebook, and she ended up being the first friend who never knew me as a guy. I had worked it out so that whenever we hung out I was in girl mode. Plus, soon after we met, I decided to officially transition which meant no more boy mode ever. In fact, it meant any new friends I made would never have a chance to meet old me. But of all the people in my life who had only ever known me as a girl, Jessica was the first. Something about that made me warm and happy.

Jessica and I became fast friends, our bond cemented by trips to Economy Candy for rare German Haribo gummies, a dressed-to-the nines night out at an adult prom party, and a mutual love of tiny food videos on Instagram. The latter of these led us to begin creating our own miniature foodstuffs: tiny mouse-sized cakes, apple pies, burgers and tacos, all accurate and edible. We did what friends do. We hung out, shared meals, talked over drinks, partied, and had adventures. Jessica was at our Thanksgiving table. We were starting to plan out-of-town trips together. One time when she came over I offered her free rein of my closet (secretly happy that I no longer had boy clothes hanging in it). We were good friends, great friends.

In fact, we became such great friends that one day she texted 'I love you', leaving me completely and utterly at a loss for how to respond. It's not uncommon for me to encounter situations where I am unsure of an appropriate response. Usually, when I get a text about someone's grandmother dying, or a co-worker announces that they are having a baby, I will consult with my partner and ask her what the appropriate response is (in this case, 'sorry for your loss' and 'congratulations'). But 'I love you' was new territory.

Guys don't say 'I love you' to their friends. They barely say it to their own spouses or children. It's such a cliché, but it's how men are socialised in our society. Emotions, men are told, are weakness (except for anger, obviously). Having been socialised male, I still carried that now-innate behaviour with me. Though so many of my friendships had been with girls, transition had provided me with my first true girl–girl friendship. This level of open affection was an unexplored land that was both enticing and foreboding.

My social and linguistic inventory held no response to something like an 'I love you' text. Love was a word that I had reserved for my partner and my partner only. How does one respond to such a thing? The classic 'I love you too' seems so obvious but it also sounds like something you'd say to a romantic partner. 'I love you too' felt wrong, not quite cheating but dressed up in the clothing of infidelity. There was the red heart emoji, but that seemed lacklustre. Sure, it was just a friend, but someone had dropped the L-word. They had told me that they cared about me, that I was important to them. Surely it should earn a better response than a tiny Unicode drawing of a heart icon.

I cursed my stupid Y chromosome that had left me assigned and raised as a male, socialised to be emotionally withdrawn and unable to show affection for a genuine friend. Just for good measure, I also cursed the testosterone poisoning that had left my body riddled with male secondary sexual characteristics. Stupid body. I made a mental note to sue it for emotional damages.

Then I thought of a middle ground. The middle path, it's the Buddhist way, right? Instead of outright typing 'I love you' or 'I love you too', I searched through the text app's gifs for one that adequately conveyed the idea without encroaching into cheat-ishy linguistic territory. Quickly, I was able to find a perfect one. It was a short gif of actress Rachel McAdams doing the classic I love you sign; pointing to herself, then making a finger heart shape on her chest, and then finally pointing to the viewer. It was perfect. It said 'I love you' without my having to actually type the phrase myself. Perfect, albeit a tad cowardly.

During the last arctic blast that left the city's temperature hovering around zero with a wind-chill of negative 10F, both Jessica and I ended up with serious cabin fever. It was cold, it was dark and we were both feeling the seasonal affective disorder hit us with a depressing vengeance. One night she texted me an emphatic message that she had to get out of the house and recommended, perhaps pleaded could be the word, that we needed to go out for a drink. As I was feeling the same way I eagerly agreed. Getting out of the house was necessary for my continued sanity.

We found a bar with a roaring fire and grabbed a spot at the back. As we huddled around the light and warmth of the flames, drinks in hand, our conversation drifted from frivolities to important topics; our own insecurities, where our upbringings might have gone wrong, hopes, fears, our thoughts on the great existential questions of life. It was a wonderful moment to share with a friend. And as it got late, after we had debated that one last round, we bid each other goodbye. With a hug, Jessica said, 'I love you,' and I replied 'I love you'. Above all else, I wanted her know that she was important to me and that her friendship was something that I treasured. Socialisation be damned.

Love is a terrible word because we ask too much of it. We want to use it to express romantic devotion, ravenous lust, appreciation for food or music, familial connection, and the strong bonds of true friendship. We casually use it all the time and yet we also save it for special occasions. And when and how to use the word is another of those unexpected things about transition. When I transitioned, I was looking forward to finally being able to present as who I really was, but I never thought a by-product of that would be letting myself have stronger bonds with my friends. I never thought transition would mean texting back 'I love you'.

EXPRESSION OF LOVE

~~~~~~

Mick

I have a simple 'armchair' theory about how and why the expression of love, particularly between parent and child, may have developed over time, as our society has. Here it is.

A few hundred years ago, people married and started families for somewhat different reasons than they do nowadays. In the olden days, marriages drew monies, increased farmsteads and were more often arranged or expected as social situations demanded. Similarly, many children were born for reasons, perhaps to contribute to work and earnings for the poorer classes or to continue the line for the wealthier classes. Birth control was non-existent until relatively recently, while infant and child mortality rates were relatively high. Parenting babies and young children a few hundred years ago would have demanded different capabilities and perhaps a stiffer upper lip than nowadays.

While I'm sure that mothers and fathers have always loved

their children, they may not have expressed their love in the ways we do now. As society developed over time, then the reasons for children became less based on the practical and perhaps more based on the fulfilment needs of adults. For example, in the 1600s, I wonder how many siblings were born with the primary purpose of being a sibling rather than another useful pair of hands. As time has gone by and society has developed, children down through the generations have had their parents' love expressed to them more and likewise have been more able to express their love towards their parents. I notice this difference when I compare my childhood and my own children's childhoods.

Let me turn now to my own story. I think that many of my parents' generation were born, under the shadow of the Second World War, into frugality and practicality – perhaps even grew up with the notion that their conception was part of the 'war effort'. Expressions of love for that generation may have reflected the social expectations of frugality and practicality, that is to say, it was expressed enough, but no more. I knew that my parents loved me and that I loved them, but I'm quite sure that the expression of that love – both ways – was stilted. I remember silence filling spaces in real life, while books and TV programmes seemed to be filled with characters who could say what needed to be said. I know that I was not alone in this regard and that many of my friends grew up this way, children of parents belonging to the war generation, perhaps also of those who didn't find the liberation of the 1960s.

So, I'd say that when I was growing up almost 50 years ago (also in a very different place from Brighton), our expressions of love in families and among friends were hugely different from what I see nowadays; they were much less outspoken.

So what? Does being able to express our love make us better people? Well, I think perhaps so, and this is why.

I look at my son, and wonder how it is that he is able to express himself so clearly as a transgender person. While I'm not transgender myself, I don't think I even got to such thoughts as a kid or, perhaps more to the point, there was no way that I would have been able to formulate such thoughts and communicate them to my parents. The expression of love that exists today between parents and their children (and in many facets of modern society) is the highway that allows young people to further express themselves, be that as transgender in my story, or in any other way, even just 'simple' emotions or feelings. In stark comparison, my childhood was closer to the 'seen and not heard' stereotype, whereas children nowadays are on a much more equal footing with adults. In my childhood, it was the norm that children's thoughts and feeling were validated by their adults, whereas nowadays children do not experience this adult-driven validation when they communicate. We inherently believe our children more nowadays than we did at any time in the past. I claim no credit for this difference; I'm merely fitting in with the society I live in. If love is unexpressed between parent and child then there's no highway to carry the important things. These things may then not be realised or even considered. Love is also being able to trust, to depend on, and to share safely with.

There have been times in my life when other people have perhaps expressed their love to me in ways that didn't suit me. I remember the very strong feeling of guilt when rebuffing misguided love, because I'd not been the person that the other wanted me to be. I have wondered about that feeling, and if it compares to my son's feelings when we (as parents) told him we loved him, and his reluctance to express his love to us – perhaps not feeling inside that he was the person we presumed him to be.

Some of our friends (and I think a significant proportion of the general population) wonder why there are 'so many' transgender young people nowadays. More broadly, I also see 'many' gay young people, 'many' young people with apparent confidence, 'many' young people not intimidated by their parents' generation and 'many' more differences between the young people today and the young people of my own generation. I believe that parents' expressions of love towards their children and greater recognition of their children's unconditional love for them has contributed to allowing young people to explore and recognise truth for themselves and then to speak about it.

I watch my kids playing 'rough and tumble' with each other, as rough as they dare be without hurting themselves or each other. To me this seems to be a natural way for them to develop trust, as they are exposing themselves to vulnerability and learning to care. I imagine that among children, this type of play has always existed no matter how developed our society is. Does this mean that it is natural for children to express their love? Perhaps our society is developing in this respect to a point where we 'allow' our kids to express their love to us, their parents, in a similar way to that which they find so natural among themselves. It would be nice to think that if this is the case then future generations will consist of people who are intrinsically more at ease with themselves and their surroundings, hand-in-hand with ultimate levels of acceptance of each other.

THE BENDS

~~~~~~

Kaoru Sato

The bar master and the lone waitress greeted me loudly as I entered. It took a while for my eyesight to adjust to the dark interior after the snowy walk in bright afternoon sun from the train station, where I'd parked my rental car. The *tachinomi* bar was small and fogged by smoke from the grill and the patrons' cigarettes. It might have squeezed in 15 people, five at the bar, the rest standing, their drinks and food perched on the narrow shelf that ran along the back wall, above which was arrayed a range of faded photos of food items, with labels and prices in messy Japanese script beneath.

It wasn't busy though. Nothing in this town seemed too busy.

I sat on a stool at the opposite end of the worn red formica bar from a middle-aged man smoking and slurping a bowl of *udon*. He glanced at me but didn't seem that interested and turned back to the sumo on the TV bolted above his end of the bar. The master was busy chopping something in the small kitchen area behind and to the side of the bar. I stuck two thousand yen on the tray in front of me as the waitress approached and I ordered a draft beer, some *yakitori* and pickled *rakkyo* shallots. She shouted the order to the master who gave a shout of assent in return.

I watched as the master poured my beer and stuck two skewers of chicken and *negi* onion on the grill. Apart from him and the waitress, the smoking man and one furtive-looking couple stood at the shelf behind me, the bar was deserted. I glanced around, wondering how to proceed with my enquiries. Above the bar was a sign that read, in English, 'Welcome. Cold food. Warm beer. Terrible service.' There was American rock and roll and biker memorabilia stuck to the walls around the sign, among which was a picture of what looked like a younger version of the master, in biker gear, standing, smiling, in front of the Grand Canyon.

The master leaned over the bar and put my beer down by me with a friendly word of offering. The glass was so cold that there was still ice stuck to the rim, which I wiped off before taking a sip. I could see him turning my *yakitori* before dipping them into a jar of dark marinade and returning them to the hot grill. They sizzled and a sweet smoke invaded the wet air.

Momentarily they were done and placed before me on a small plate with a garnish of lettuce and chopped, vinegared cucumber. At the same time, the waitress appeared by my side with a metal side dish of sweet pickled *rakkyo* and took the bills from my tray, leaving me almost a thousand in change.

I was grateful for the drink and hot, richly flavoured food after my morning-long drive up through the mountain roads from New Chitose Airport. I ordered another *yakitori* portion and got out my phone, finding the photos of Mā-chan I'd saved on the device.

The first photo had been taken when we were both at junior

high school in the western suburb of Tokyo where we grew up. I remembered that day well. We'd both been members of the 'Speaking English' club at school and we had been on an excursion to Kawasaki to take part in an inter-school competition that involved delivering three-minute speeches we had written in the language. They were to be judged by a panel including a quite famous English academic who had settled in Tokyo and become something of a 'celebrity expert' on Japanese culture. He appeared a lot on panel shows on Japanese TV.

My speech topic was on soccer. I wasn't confident.

I remember being really impressed by Mā-chan's topic. He had written a short sequel to the Charles Dickens story, A *Christmas Carol*, imagining an unexpected death in the Cratchit family the summer following, and relating how Scrooge had called down the Christmas spirits one more time to grant the grieving Mrs Cratchit and her children one last conversation with her late husband.

I was convinced he was going to win. He delivered his declamation beautifully in the school hall where the contest was held. His English even then was very good and he especially captured Mrs Cratchit's sadness as he related his tale to the hushed crowd.

He had been subdued after the winners were announced and he didn't get a place. But we were soon fooling around on the train back again, when my dad snapped the photo of us caught in mid laugh on the seat in a shaft of late spring afternoon sunshine. I was looking out of the window and Mā-chan was leaning on me with his slender arms raised, probably acting out one of the Christmas spirits' comical annoyance at being woken in the heat of a Victorian London summer. We would have been 15.

The second photo was from ten years later.

We'd been best friends for years and had followed our joint dream (at considerable cost to our parents) to go to university in Britain. Mā-chan (or Masao as we referred to him by then, using his full name) had got a spot to take Fine Art at the prestigious Goldsmiths College. I was studying for a Bachelor's in International Relations at the London School of Economics. We'd met frequently in our first year, but had found ourselves drifting apart as our interests and circles of friends had shifted. By then I'd met and begun living with my future wife, Caroline, in the second year. Masao didn't seem to have much luck with relationships. I saw him with a string of frighteningly bohemian girls but none seemed to remain for long. Our meetings, too, would become fleeting and ever more spaced out.

The photo was from the last time I saw him in Britain. It was at the private view of a group show in which he was participating, at a warehouse space somewhere in the wilds of East London. I remember that Caroline and I had been shocked by the change in him – we'd not seen him for a year or so. He was almost skeletally gaunt, draped in androgynous-looking black clothes, with long hair down to his waist and a far-off expression which I learned later was probably related to a severe drugs habit. 'He looks like a vampire,' she whispered to me.

The photo that Caroline took that night shows him gazing past the camera with a fixed intensity, at an indeterminate middle distance. The bright light of the setting sun catches one eye, rendering it almost iris-less. One scrawny, bangle encrusted arm, cigarette in hand, is draped around my stiff shoulders. I'm smiling at the camera but look profoundly uncomfortable.

As we said our goodbyes that night, he'd hugged me and said, in Japanese (we'd spoken in English all evening), 'Let's meet up again soon, just you and me. I miss the old days.' I'd hugged him back and repeated, 'Yes. Soon'.

I never saw him in England again, and have only seen him once, since. I found out he'd gone home to Japan a few weeks after the show had finished. For good.

I drained the beer and took another bite of chicken, looking for another thousand-yen bill to place in the pot. I called for the waitress and she appeared momentarily by my seat. I ordered another beer and a bowl of *kitsune udon*. After she'd shouted out the order, I noticed her looking over my shoulder at my phone screen, which still showed the photo of the older, 'vampire' Masao. Then another customer called and she drifted away to serve them.

Outside it was getting dark as the winter sun began to dip towards the horizon. My hot noodles and cold beer arrived and I began slurping both down. Unnoticed, the other customers had slipped out into the icy street and I was alone in the bar. The waitress finished clearing and wiping the plates then got her coat from behind the bar. She spent a while wrapping herself up against the cold then gave me a polite 'thank you' and left the shop with a shout to the master, who was reading a newspaper and occasionally stirring the *oden* hotpot permanently simmering away behind the bar. He grunted a farewell at her.

I waited until I eventually caught his eye and said, 'It'll be cold tonight.'

'The winter's come early this year,' he agreed, in a non-committal but not unfriendly way. 'Another beer?'

I nodded and watched as he served me up another glass of Sapporo. I continued the conversational dance while continuing to slurp my noodles. 'I flew in from Tokyo this morning. Hard to believe it's still warm autumn down there.'

'Ah, it never really gets cold in Tokyo though,' he said, smiling. 'But what brings you all the way up north to our mountain country?'

'Actually,' I replied, choosing my words slowly and carefully, 'I came looking for a friend from Tokyo. They went missing a year ago.' I switched my phone screen back on and prepared, once again, to show my friend's face to a stranger.

It wasn't for another three or four years after that last meeting that I saw Masao again. He was living quietly back at his mother's house in Kinuta, the leafy suburb of Tokyo where we'd grown up. He'd got a job in a local convenience store. On a family summer trip back to sweltering Tokyo with Caroline and our son, I made time to visit and found him to be quieter, less dissociated. Still very thin, he seemed less troubled, perhaps. He had a stillness about him. Maybe a resignedness. 'I've kicked the drugs,' he leaned over and told me over ice tea that afternoon. 'I feel that I can begin to see a way ahead now. Past the bends in the road.' He'd frequently lapse into awkward silences, as if his eyes were turned inwards, surveying a complex and dimly understood interior landscape. He asked enthusiastically about my life in London with my wife and child and promised he'd be back to visit once he'd saved enough money.

I asked if he was still making art. He smiled and shook his head after a long silence. 'That is no longer part of the way ahead for me.' He shook his head again, as though knocking some loose piece back into place, and lapsed back into silence.

His mother cooked us dinner. She told me, when Masao went to smoke in his room, that she hadn't seen him so happy and calm since he'd been back and that she hoped I'd visit again soon. I said I would be sure to visit any time I was in Japan.

Later, as I departed into the humid, cicada-filled Tokyo night for the Odakyu line station, he trotted after me, brushed my bare forearm with his hand to stop me. I was seized by a desperate nostalgia. It was a gesture he'd used a lot after school, when his racing imagination reminded him of something he had to tell me about after we'd parted. As he stood in front of me in the light of the full moon, it seemed to me that he'd regressed into the Mā-chan of high school; full of the future and ready to change into something unknown and marvellous.

'Let's meet up again, soon, just you and me,' he told me earnestly, 'I miss the old days.' I touched him gently on the shoulder and repeated, 'Yes. Soon.'

The bar master hadn't seen him of course. No one had, in any of the places I'd thought to search for my missing friend.

After his mother died, a few months after my visit – unbeknown to me she had already been carrying the cancer in her bowel that was to kill her – Masao had lived in the house on his own for a number of years. Then all of a sudden, he'd sold the house and vanished. The first I'd heard of it was an email from his cousin, whom I barely knew, asking whether Masao was with me in London. I then realised that I'd not received any of his rambling and irregular emails for some time. I'd had other things on my mind. My marriage had been breaking up and Caroline and I were finally divorced a couple of months before I received the email.

After a fruitless correspondence with various family members, most of whom seemed relieved that the black sheep had finally wandered away from the flock, I decided vaguely to use an upcoming holiday to try and find Masao. So, autumn found me landing back at Narita with no plan, three weeks and few hundred thousand yen with which to conduct the search.

I first tried the police in Kinuta, who were polite but unhelpful.

They suggested that if I or a family member wished to report him missing they could look into it, but without much conviction. The internet hinted that an artist by his name was working at a mountain studio in Okutama, a very remote, mountainous part of Western Tokyo. There was no answer by email or landline so I spent a few exhausting days driving around the area, first locating the art studio, which turned out have been abandoned years before, then showing Mā-chan's photo round restaurants, bars and tourist offices in various towns and villages in the region to no avail. I drove my rental car back home to the city through the beautiful autumn countryside, drained and despondent.

It was while shopping for a late-night drink and snack at a convenience store the night of my return that I remembered that Mā-chan had worked at such a place. No one at the store I was in knew of him, but I worked my way round all the local ones and eventually found the one where he had worked, a FamilyMart slightly away from Kinuta's main station drag. The night manager remembered him well. 'He was a good person, hard worker, but there was something missing. I don't know. Like he'd lost his way.' I asked if he knew at all where Mā-chan might have gone. He shrugged. 'He talked about Hokkaido a couple of times. I guess you could lose yourself there. Big place and not much there.'

A blinding light turned on in my head and I thanked him and hurried out. Mā-chan had, a few years ago, shared a photo album with me of a remote mountain town in the vast interior of Japan's northern island whose simplicity seemed to have touched him in some inexplicable way. To me it had looked like any shabby, small, rural, mountain town. I ran home to my Airbnb, certain that that link to the album in the gmail thread I had kept with him would lead me to my friend.

I was now no longer that certain. After leaving the bar I'd tramped round the town all night showing the photo to shopkeepers, barmen, waiters and passers-by, but no one had seen or heard of Masao. I'd enquired at the local *kōban* police box and been advised that I should make a report at the police station in Asahikawa, the nearest large town, 70 kilometres away. Now I was sat in my hire car drinking a tin of warm vending machine coffee in the freezing night, by the deserted rail station. The snow had stopped but an icy chill had set in. Everything seemed hopeless. I was prepared to give it all up and begin the long drive back to the warmth of my hotel room in Sapporo city.

Then a small figure, treading cautiously on the black ice, crossed the front of my car, making towards the station bus stop. I saw it pause, turn and peer in at me.

It was the waitress, no doubt returning from her evening shift at the bar. She walked round to my door. I looked stupidly up at her. I was very tired. Impatiently she tapped on the glass with her mittened hand. I lowered the window.

'The boss says you were looking for Mā-chan. Give me a lift home and I can help you.'

Her name was Hiroko. She lived in a small block of flats in the outskirts of the town. I'd explained my quest to her in the car and she'd listened in silence. 'Come up and have a drink, if you want,' she said, trudging wearily up the metal stairs with a bag of shopping. 'Boss didn't know you were looking for Mā-chan really. He just told me some strange man from Tokyo was looking for a missing friend. But I saw that photo too, remember?' In her small, bare apartment, she poured me a whisky and we sat on cushions on the *tatami* floor. We were still in our coats. The aircon was taking a while to heat up the room. I watched her as she sipped her drink and smoked a menthol cigarette. She was older than she'd looked in the dim light of the bar. Tired looking, but pretty, with shortish hair in a side parting, the longer side tucked behind one ear. A small, star-shaped stud glinted in her exposed lobe. She looked up at me, observing my face. We sat in silence for a moment.

'How much did you really know your friend, do you think?' she said suddenly.

I shrugged, 'I knew him well when we were kids. But the longer I knew him the less I knew him, I guess.' I trailed off. She nodded. Again, there was silence. 'Just a minute,' she said, springing lightly to her feet and opening the sliding screen into the bedroom next door. She returned with an iPad, which she powered up.

'Mā-chan arrived here last summer. I was looking for a flatmate and we got on when we met in the bar so we ended up living here together.' I could barely contain myself but I let her continue, taking my coat off. She had already removed hers and shoved her legs into the kotatsu under-table heater. 'This is a picture of us outside here last autumn.' She passed me the tablet.

For a moment, I wanted to go through the motions, to say that she had made a mistake, but in reality, I knew that the black clad woman standing next to Hiroko in the photo was Mā-chan. She was tall for a Japanese woman, but not freakishly so. She looked happy, striking, and more confident than I'd seen for a long time, perhaps since Masao had given that speech in that competition so many years ago.

'Did Mā-chan...,' I began, still looking down at the image on the screen. Hiroko interrupted me.

'Yes. She told me about you. She talked about you a lot. Mā-chan loved you, so much, but didn't feel she could be with you as she was. That you would be revolted by her.'

I felt a crushing weight envelop my head, and then slowly rise away, like colour draining from fabric that was being bleached. I couldn't speak, but finally looked up from the screen into Hiroko's wide eyes, as though I was trying to push all the questions bubbling up from my head into hers.

Hiroko's calm, quiet voice continued. 'Being transgender is really hard in Japan, I found out from her. Her life was unbelievably difficult. She made ends meet by doing webcam shows in her bedroom and escort work in Asahikawa. But I also found that she'd been looking at internet sites and social network groups about suicide.' She paused, lighting another cigarette, gesturing upwards with it. 'One evening this March, I came home and found her hanging from that beam in the ceiling.'

A cold certainty had solidified round my heart as Hiroko had gone on. I found that my face was wet with tears.

She took my hand. 'You should stay here tonight. You can't drive back to Sapporo in this ice.'

The next morning, I rose early, folded away the futon she'd put out for me in the living area, dressed quietly and made to leave, but noticed suddenly that Hiroko was awake in the dim bedroom beyond the half-open screen, looking at me with her big, dark eyes. She reached quickly beneath her pillow, like a bird catching a worm, and pulled out the iPad. 'You should have this. It belonged to her. It has all her photos and stuff on it.'

Dumbly I reached out and took it, nodding.

Hiroko went on, 'If you want to feel some connection with Mā-chan, there's a place you might want to go, before heading back to the city.'

I pushed the nose of the car higher up the switchback bends towards the secluded mountain valley. Hiroko had told me that

Mā-chan would often come to this place. The valley floor was thin, she'd said, and the underworld broke through easily. She went there to feel closer to that other world. As the car crested the final ridge, I saw it spread below me, and the smell of sulphur hit me at the same time. The valley was pockmarked with volcanic vents, the ground an unnatural orange hue. Vegetation half dead, yet clinging on despite the unusual cold of that late November and the dry heat of the sulphurous smoke.

This place hadn't featured in the photos Mā-chan had sent me years ago. Perhaps she'd not discovered it yet. Or perhaps it was too special to her. So many questions. But first.

Hiroko had told me that there was a place in the valley that Mā-chan particularly valued. I pulled up by the roadside, certain I'd found it. A bubbling lake spread out before me, heated by geothermal energy. The car was soon enveloped in warm steam. Signs warned anyone foolhardy enough to try and take a dip, of water temperatures that would scald the skin from their flesh.

Beside the boiling lake was a stand of maple, twisted out of shape by the extreme conditions, but still thriving. Beyond, white-topped mountains rose up into the clear blue sky. I walked into the maple copse, snow crisp beneath my feet, sulphur burning my lungs. The path meandered through the gnarled trees, and leaves dried by heat crunched, red, under my boots.

Presently the trees opened up and the whole view presented itself. The sulphurous valley tumbling and spitting away below, the lake seething ahead of me, the mountains and sky, in their pristine, cold majesty above. Hell, purgatory and heaven, pushing together through the skin between worlds, here where it was thinnest; the most stretched.

All I could do was stand and watch it for a while.

Then I felt the faintest of vibrations in the air around me, as though a slight presence was trying weakly to push sideways through the gaps between the worlds. I thought I could see a faint, bluish-green ball of light in the distance, flitting among the steam and smoke above the lake. It never came any closer but I felt it pushing against the contours of my awareness nevertheless.

I said, quietly, in my head, 'Mā-chan, is that you?'

I felt the vibration grow slightly stronger for a moment, and the ball of light brightened a little. It now felt as if she was standing next to me in the clearing. I reached out and felt my friend lightly touch my forearm, like I had before on that warm night in Tokyo.

'Let's meet up again, soon, just you and me,' I said. 'I miss the old days.' She touched me gently on the shoulder and repeated, 'Yes. Soon.'

♡

ON LOVE – WHAT WE LOVE

Tell me about someone, or something you love

I love my wife, my rock through all the hard times. Dating someone who is transitioning can't be easy, but she married me anyway.

She has this glance in her eyes when she smiles… But there's no chance for me to become her partner, for she's hetero. It's like my heart got stabbed with a red but very thorny rose.

I really love the people who supported me and understand me. It is hard to find people, who say, 'Yes, I know how you feel.' I want to hug them.

I love music, especially singing. I have a crush on a person right now and love many details about them, but I don't know them well enough to say I love the whole person. I love a group of friends I'm working on a project with.

Right now, I love my cat who is lying snoozing beside me. She teaches me a lot about consent because she makes it very clear what she wants and doesn't want, and she teaches me about loving the vulnerable parts of myself and others.

I've loved one person for a very long time now and that love has changed its meaning over the years.

My mum. She gives me the most perfect and beautiful unconditional love I could ever ask for. She supports me through everything, even things that she may not fully understand. She is my best friend, my teammate, always at my side, fighting for me.

I love BDSM (bondage, discipline (or domination), sadism, and masochism) and kink play. I would even go so far as to say that my sexuality and even a large part of my identity are inextricably linked to BDSM. I find that consensual power and sensory play really help me to make deep connections with my own body and help me to manage my dysphoria. I really love the sense of joyful play and I have found that I can use it to process some of my trauma. I love to learn and share.

My dog. What an angel.

My partner. He is such a wonderful human and I couldn't see myself without the love I have for him. I also love my books...

My wife. It's not just that we've been together forever, it's also that we've shared so many experiences. She knew I was non-binary before I did and she knows me well enough to give me space to figure it out for myself (because I almost instinctively vehemently oppose labels other people give me).

Can't remember.

I still love my ex-girlfriend, she means the world to me.

Alex is just the most beautiful boy. I adore him eternally.

I still love my dog, despite the fact he ain't with us anymore.

I'm fond of many things but haven't got anyone or thing that is the total source of my adoration.

My boyfriend is the obvious one, but I also love my sons beyond words. I'm not sure if it will last with my boyfriend though. It feels like hard work.

I love my family, both blood and chosen. They are the people who keep me going, who encourage me. They fight for me and care for me when I'm feeling weak. They love me unconditionally and I'd be lost without them.

I love ceramics – none of the tableware I use matches; each unique piece is made by individual artists. Each piece is loved for how it feels to the touch and how it makes me feel each time I choose to use it.

I love my boyfriend so much. He is the kindest, most sensitive person I know.

I love my 2-year-old, who has seen me change and knows his body and my body and sees that they are different and the same. Who loves Barbies and Batman and insists I paint his nails if I do mine and then goes off to fight imaginary crime. I have hope that I can show him the spectrum that gender is so he will never feel like he has to hide whatever he feels inside and if one day he tells me that he isn't a boy, we'll discover his identity together and I won't let my child feel like it's a lonely road, which it has been for so many trans people in the past, myself included. I will fight tooth and nail for my children's right to be who they want to be and I will destroy any boxes that others try to shove them in.

My granddaughter. She's working on her psychology degree so we can research together on some disorders we share.

My oldest friend, my best friend, my once lover, a relationship so complex and important that words don't work for it and we have to talk in cat. And also, one of my partners, a magic and gentle creature who wandered into my life a year ago, and to whom I can say anything and feel totally free.

I'm still in love with the girl I met 27 years ago. She was my soulmate when I met her; even now after all the pain I have caused her I know she is still my soulmate and my love still runs as deep. She always will be my soulmate.

I love my sister. We tried to kill each other as siblings do, but in the last two years she has really become my champion, asserting my pronouns and identity to me and our parents. She recognises my struggles with mental health and makes space for me to feel good when I visit our loud family.

PART 5

SELF-LOVE

I've never really thought of myself as a quitter. I like to think that once I go for something, I'm there for the long haul, like a dog with a log, never letting go, all focus channelled into the task at hand.

The thing is, over the last few years, I've realised this is sort of true, but not always in a good way.

Yeah, I'm tenacious, but often it's only in relation to hopeless situations.

That no-quit attitude? Only there when it comes to putting myself down and chipping away at my own self-esteem.

And being overwhelmingly focused on the task at hand? Well, yes, if the task at hand is taking on everything negative that happens to me as being a fault with me.

Yeah, I'm very good at not quitting when it comes to things I hate.

I think if many of us were honest with ourselves, we'd probably have similar experiences.

If you break up with someone, say, it's hard not to see fault in yourself. In fact, quite often the other person in the relationship will help you with that as well, and by help I obviously mean offer up a brutal character assassination uniquely tailored for you.

I know my self-esteem can be a fragile thing. It's as if it's made of ice – any heat will melt it pretty fast, and god help us all if you go for it with a hammer. I try and build it up as best I can, but after a while it starts to become the norm that it will melt away, and once that happens it becomes much harder to sort it out.

I think that's because there's comfort in repetition, even if it's negative repetition. Doing the same thing, having the same response is safe because it's familiar. It almost doesn't matter that it hurts you more, that it's ultimately incredibly self-destructive, because at least you know this feeling. There is security and safety because it's what you know.

Look at it like a rollercoaster. The first time you go on it, its frankly fucking terrifying: 'I'm gonna be sick, what's happening, *I can not deal with this.*' But then you go on it again, and again, and again, and after a while you know all the twists, you remember the bit where you go upside down where you feel sick, and you get used to it. The more you do it, the easier it becomes to keep on doing it, even if it keeps on making you feel sick.

The familiarity of thinking negatively about myself is often an easier route to take than stopping and thinking about whether it's actually true or not. For example, for a long time I was pretty sure that the only way I could ever experience love was by not acknowledging that I was trans.

We're talking all love here as well.

I thought my family would disown me if I told them I was trans. I didn't think my partner at the time would understand, I thought our relationship would be done if I transitioned. I thought that if my relationship did end I'd die alone, as I'd be unlovable if I acknowledged my transness.

And, of course, there's the fact that I certainly didn't love myself. It's kind of ironic I know, that in order to experience love I ended up not loving anything.

I think I knew I was trans for a very long time. I also quickly learned from an early age though that knowing something is one thing, and doing something about it is an entirely different thing.

I'd seen people who were different being bullied and ostracised at school, and I'd heard adults talking about not drawing attention to yourself and conforming if you wanted to get anywhere in life. I saw that if you had something different about you, and others saw that, then things would go badly for you.

And for me, growing up in the eighties, things were already pretty bad. You how earlier I said I knew I was trans? Well, it's a bit more complicated than that.

Back then I was missing a fundamental thing that would have helped me.

Language.

I had no words to describe how I felt. I couldn't research stuff on the internet because it didn't exist. I couldn't find any books, or magazine articles about who I was because there were none (or if there were, they weren't accessible to me).

I couldn't get involved with anything that might or might not have been going on in any scene because I was barely a teenager. I was chronically shy, and even if I wasn't I had no idea where to look, because I didn't have any words to describe how I was.

I was a singular world of me. Alone, with no one I could talk to, and no words to describe who I was even if there was someone. For a long time, I thought I was the only one like me, and I knew that being the only one of something didn't end well once other people realised.

I wish I had been born into a different time, or that I had more confidence, and had found a way to express what I felt. I wish that I'd had more tools to navigate this, or someone I could trust with who I was. I wish all this, but I also know that these are dead-end wishes.

I was still a child back then and the only tools I had were simple and blunt, so I did the only thing I could. I buried who I was and tried to be 'normal'.

My thinking was if I acted normal then I would be someone people could love, and maybe if I kept at it then this glitch inside me might go away.

Maybe it was just a thing that would pass. Maybe I just needed to sit it out. Maybe if I just pretended it was not happening then it would go away.

Yeah.

So a lot of time went by and I did normal things like have a relationship, get married and buy a house, and it didn't go away. Funnily enough, what actually happened is that I ended up hating myself more and more, because I knew what I needed to do, but I knew also that the cost of doing what I needed to do was so high that I didn't think I could bear it.

And then the internet happened and everything changed. Before the internet, I had seen glimpses of people like me. At first there was nothing, but as time went on, and we started heading into the nineties, the glimpses became more frequent.

There were the films and television series with trans characters. They were nearly always portrayed in a negative way (the villain in *Ace Ventura*, the serial killer in *Silence of the Lambs*, Chandler's constantly mocked parent in *Friends*, for example) but there was also an occasional glimmer of positivity in films like *Orlando*.

Very occasionally, I'd read a magazine article about a trans person, or how gender fluidity was this new underground thing, but these were few and far between.

I was searching for proof that I was not alone, like an astronomer scanning the skies for signs of other life, but not wanting to send out any signals of her own in case the life she finds is hostile to her world.

Like I said, glimpses, but little that was positive and nothing that was like me, or how I felt.

And then I got the internet. Of course, I searched. The desire, some might even say hunger, to find people like you is a strong one, and I'd seen glimpses that there might be others like me, so suddenly the chances of life seemed more likely.

Inevitably a lot of what I found at first was porn. The internet is what it is, and porn was, and still is, a predominant feature. A lot of it focused on transvestite narratives but it was a start, and when you're looking for something on the internet all you need is one word for the doors to start to open.

I searched and discovered other people. Like me. I read their stories and saw I wasn't alone. I saw that some of these people were exactly like me. Knowing it's not just you can be one of the most powerful forces for change in the world.

I saw that other people like me were living as their true selves. They were being authentic, and, yes, sometimes it was tough, but they had survived and, more than that, they were okay.

I cannot emphasise enough how enormous it is to know that you're not alone, and that even more so, you can be okay.

Seeing other trans people being true to who they were gave me the strength to come out, and to start the very long journey to loving myself.

I could have that love, others had found it, and if they could, so could I.

So, what of those fears I mentioned at the start?

I thought my family would disown me if I told them I was trans

I'm going to say right away that this wasn't easy. My parents truggled. It was obvious and apparent to me that they really struggled, as much as they tried to hide it.

The thing is, though, they also tried. Sometimes they fucked up, by dead-naming me (using the name you were assigned at birth rather than your chosen name) or by misgendering me. And yes, when they did that it really fucking hurt. (As they say, you don't have a therapist for the lols.)

But they did try. They read books about being trans. They watched documentaries and films and tried to learn what all these new words meant. They tried as best they could, and really, that's all you can ask anyone to do. I've been living with this for my whole life while they had only just begun, and as much as sometimes I wished they'd just try that little bit harder, maybe in hindsight that's exactly what they were doing.

I didn't think my partner at the time would understand, I thought our relationship would be done if I transitioned

Again, this was not easy. As you can probably see, there's a theme forming here. So first, my worst fear did ring true. Our romantic relationship ended the day I came out as trans. But, looking back, our relationship was over a long time before that. We'd been together a long time, and during that time we'd discovered that actually we wanted different things from life, and those things weren't compatible. We didn't stop loving each other, but we did realise that we needed to let each other go if both of us wanted to live our fullest lives.

We are still good friends ten years later, and honestly us breaking up was the best thing we did for each other. The only thing I regret about that time is not being honest sooner.

I thought that if my relationship did end that I'd die alone, as I'd be unlovable if I acknowledged my transness

So, putting aside the melodrama of dying alone for one moment, this turned out to be so not true. It seems that being true to yourself makes you really fucking hot to a lot of people.

Yes, as I've mentioned before, there is a lot of fear and prejudice in the dating scene towards trans people, but it's also clear from speaking to anyone who has dated people that we as trans people are not alone in this. The dating scene is a hot mess of fear and prejudice.

I've been single and in relationships since coming out as trans, and sometimes it's been great, and sometimes it's been not so great, but there have been, and still are, people who have loved me.

I am fucking lovable, despite being trans, and that's really, really great.

I certainly didn't love myself

Honestly, this is a lifetime's work. Loving myself is by far the hardest thing I've ever done, because everything tells me not to. It takes effort and persistence, and a lot of therapy. (Once again, I find myself repeating – you don't have a therapist for the lols.)

Thing is though, I do love myself a lot more now than I did, and when you're coming from nothing that's a universe-sized improvement.

Loving yourself is the best thing you can do for you. If you only do one thing in your life it should be this. It's the most important thing in the whole world, and yet it's the one thing we all consistently neglect.

Think about it. If you truly love yourself then any extra love is a bonus. It also matters so much less when you realise that most of the love you get from other people is conditional. The armour of self-love will fill the hole that gets left behind.

Knowing that you are great, and deserving of love, and, most importantly, that that love comes from within, means that you can live an authentic life!

So you're trans. You know that your parents find that difficult. But you really love who you are. Like *really* love who you are. And you start to realise that actually, maybe your parents are just people, with their own stuff going on, and some of it might be a bit fucked up, but that's actually kind of like you in a way. And it's okay. They love you, and they express that as best they can, and yeah, at first it feels like that's just not enough, but then you remember that they are people like you, and they're doing their best, and you love yourself, and that can fill that gap, because you finally are living how you want, being who you are, being true.

The love you feel for yourself makes it okay, because you've got you. Anything else is a bonus.

Once you start to love yourself then that, in turn, starts to change your way of thinking. Obviously, I don't want to feel shit about myself every time something bad happens, so now I try to stop and think about it a little. I think about if it is really something to do with me, or if it's actually something to do with someone else, and I'm just being a sponge for their emotions. Sometimes it is me, but a lot of the time it isn't.

When I get upset because someone on Tinder can't deal with me being trans, for instance, I try not to take that as a reflection on me anymore. I try not to do that because the truth of it is that it's not me who has the problem. It's not for me to take that on, and there is no need to put myself down, because I have done nothing that is deserving of that.

It is, of course, easier to write this than do it, but self-love was never going to be easy for any of us. That's what makes it so powerful when we do start to do it.

Over the course of the following pages you'll find writing about self-love. Sometimes, as always, there's a cross-over between other types of love, but the predominant theme is how we love ourselves.

Loving yourself is hard, and it's a lifelong commitment, but it is possible. More than that, it's attainable for all of us. Sometimes it doesn't feel that way, sometimes it feels like the whole world is against you, but trust me when I say you can get there.

These are the stories of how we learned to love ourselves, despite the odds.

These are the stories of our lives.

LOVE

~~~~~~~

Ryan

Love.

It seems a very simple word. A simple word to write. At times, a simple word to say. One syllable. Four letters. It flows from the pen, rolls off the tongue. The meaning of it is not so simple...

As a man with a trans history, I have had a very complex relationship with love. Love for people, love for myself, love for my job. At every point in my life the notion of love has come with significant complexities.

At 28 years young, I wouldn't say I am worldly wise by any means; however, I would say the more time has passed, the more I have been able to understand what love means to me, in all of its forms. And let's be clear, I am still learning, discovering, adapting and understanding where love fits in all parts of my life.

Love, the word itself, seems simplistic. For me, it doesn't quite do justice to the actual feeling of love. Through my life, I have experienced what I have thought was love, what has been love and what continues to be love. Love that was felt for me and love I have felt for others. Love that was unconditional, and at times conditional.

Family love is the most complex I have experienced. When family love has been removed from you because of who you are, you can begin to lose faith in love itself, as familial love is generally the first type of love we know and experience. I remember being told by a family member that they had to force themselves to stop loving me. Their love for me became conditional because of my transition. How did I overcome this? How did I process the fact that someone who should love me unconditionally was now putting a condition on love? My choice was to not transition and be loved by my family, or to transition and not be loved. I went for the latter. Honestly, I am not sure I have ever processed this effectively. I mean, how do you process something like that?! Now, nearly ten years on and a bit of learning and growing up done in the process (by both parties!), I have a positive relationship with the person who made love conditional. Interestingly, however painful it was to not be loved, I still felt love for them. Love isn't something I believe we are able to turn off, no matter how much pain the removal, or threat of removal, can cause.

Love for myself is not something I consider much. I'm not sure if I could say I love myself. Thinking about it now is making me feel uncomfortable. It feels weird to say I love myself, in part because I'm not sure if it's true, and in part because it feels arrogant. I guess some form of love for myself may come from accepting myself, or at least beginning to. I have a mildly hostile relationship with my trans history. I am not ashamed of being trans but I am certainly not proud of it, and so by default, love for my trans self becomes a very messy area. It is painful and frustrating. It causes anger and sadness. It makes areas of my life complex and some relationships challenging. And quite frankly, it just pisses me right off at times!

So, can all of these things co-exist with loving myself? I suppose they can on some level. My experiences form parts of the way I am today so there has to be some benefit to all the shit that has come with being trans. Do I love my body? No. Do I love having to work out which public toilets will definitely lock? No. Do I love that I have to edit or omit parts of my history in case it outs me as trans? No. But there are aspects I do love. I love that I am able to use my experiences for good. I love that I am able to feel more at home in my body, even if not fully. I love that I am able to be a voice for those who have been silenced. I love that I have the absolute privilege of being a positive role model to children and young people who at times feel there is no hope. These things are how I am able to love some parts of my trans self.

I guess this leads me on to the love I have for my job. I haven't yet begun to attempt to put into words how love actually feels. I guess the love I have for my job is something I feel very physically. It is something that at times is a funny, squiggly feeling. At other times, it is much more than that.

My job is by no means easy. At times, it makes me want to pull my hair out, throw things or cry. Sometimes all on the same day! Youth work, in itself, is no easy feat. Youth work with children and young people who share your identity, and even some of your experiences, comes with additional challenges. However, this does not override the amount of love I have for what I do. You know the funny, squiggly feelings of love I mentioned before? I certainly don't experience those feelings when I look at the never-ending list of things I have to do, or when the work I do is misrepresented in national press, or when I sit in three-hour meetings that could just be discussed in an email. I do, however, experience that feeling when I meet a child for the first time and see the weight lift from their shoulders and a smile creep onto their face when I tell them that what they are feeling is okay. I experience that feeling when I am stood next to a child when they come out to their peer group, and their classmates show them the love and acceptance they so rightly deserve. I experience the funny, squiggly feelings of love more often in this role than in any other job I have had. I am proud to do the job I do. I am passionate about supporting LGBT children and young people. I will stand by them, both metaphorically and literally. I will work a 60-hour week to ensure they get the support they deserve. I will fight their corner when their school is cocking up their coming-out process, and I will just sit with them in silence if that is what they want. All of these things form the love I have for my job – the love that will not be diminished, even on those days when all I want to do is cry. This love is powerful. It is strong. It is as fierce as hell. And since 2012, it has not wavered.

It seems apt that if I am talking about love, I should speak about the romantic love I experience. More specifically, the love I have for my partner. This kind of love, on the face of it, seems simple. I tell my partner I love him. I say this almost daily and have been doing so for the past eight years. You can be sure that when I tell him I love him, I mean it with every part of my being. But does saying 'I love you' actually do the feeling of love justice? In this case, I'm not sure it does. I have mentioned a few physical feelings of love I experience, from those funny, squiggly feelings to the fierce and powerful. The love I have for my partner is a variation of these and much more.

For me, the love I have for him is tied up in so many things.

He makes me be a better person. He helps me feel confident. He is practical and logical, a fine balance for my emotionally driven nature. He is thoughtful and sensitive in ways that sometimes I overlook. He is passionate, creative and stands strong to his beliefs. He has helped me learn to trust again.

Trust is another simple word like love. Without trust I would not be able to love fully. The two are inextricably linked. I am lucky to be with someone who I fully trust and therefore can fully love.

So why have I bothered to write about why I love my partner? I suppose it informs the love I feel for him. It is less messy than other types of love I have felt. It seems more straightforward. I get those floaty butterflies in my stomach – you know, the ones when you aren't sure if you need to run around in circles with your arms in the air or lie down on the floor and take deeps breaths. My heart beats faster and louder when we talk about our plans for the future. My palms get sweaty and tingly when he is all dressed up looking beautifully handsome. All of these things and more are the physical manifestations of love that I feel for him.

I feel lucky to have such strong feelings of love that I can give to another person. Don't get me wrong, this type of love is terrifying and incredible in equal measures but to have it reciprocated is one of the best things in the world.

Love for me also has a place in the simple things in life. For example, I love sunsets. I love the countryside. I love dogs, chimpanzees and my grandma's leek and potato soup. I love looking at the stars on clear night. I love Enter Shikari's music. I love reading, gardening and swimming. All of these things have a significant place in my life. I love each of them in different ways for different reasons. Maybe it seems silly to use the word love for simple things but the use of 'love' in this context does not devalue the word itself. It is the simple things in life that can create the strongest feelings of love.

Sometimes, being a trans person, it can be easy to forget what love is depending on what our experiences are, whether that is giving or receiving love, it being conditional or unconditional, familial or romantic or the love we feel for our passions in life. Love is, in some ways, a feeling that sometimes we just can't put our finger on. Love can be static or fluid, outgoing or incoming. It can be ever changing.

Whatever love is, it continues to be a vital part of my life. And for you, reader, I hope that it is a part of yours.

UNTITLED (SINCE IT HAPPENED)

Benjamin

Since it happened
I've said your name out loud only once
I wanted to see if I could pronounce
the sound of your consonants
the shape of your vowels
could I muster my mouth?
could I find the power?

I found you on Facebook
blue eyes and blond hair
now with a little boy
smiling with daddy
happy, unaware

It seems like a lifetime ago
you wouldn't recognise me
I can hide under my skin
my maleness, my identity
like a blanket

although safer, not safe
not completely

I told someone, a friend
even though I felt shame
confronted, called out
you shifted the blame
you said 'she's lying
that's just what girls like her do'
afraid and resentful
like it was me that hurt you

It seems like a lifetime away
yet nothing has changed
my eyes are still pierced
my vision, your face
when I am dreaming
I think of your house, your street
when I hear Metallica
my heart pounds, offbeat

Your skin on my lips
the tears in my eyes
I made you look away
could I have misread the signs?
forced to repeat it
yet they could prove no crime
can I find forgiveness within me?
with this passing of time?

SELF-LOVE

We were children, really
we were fifteen
I'd hoped I would have moved past it
now that I'm twenty-three
'He probably didn't mean to'
'It was just a joke' they said
I'll try to remind myself of that
when I'm alone in my bed

There is something inside me
something charred, something black
left for dead, left behind
and can't ever come back
that thing is me
my younger self, just fifteen
that felt ruined, ignored, ashamed
and unclean

Today I stand before you
although wounded, still bleeding
despite all the times that I stopped believing
that I could be loved
that I could be safe
despite that sometimes I still see your face
I stand before you
wounded but healing
self-love is the key
self-love can be freeing.

UNTITLED

~~~~~~~~

Roch

I never loved myself before I knew who I was. At best, I tolerated myself. At worst, to put it mildly, I didn't tolerate myself.

A 'mixed-race' kid. A 'tomboy'. A weirdo. A person on the fringes, wondering why I couldn't love myself whenever I looked in the mirror. I knew something was off, but I couldn't put a finger on what it was. Like hearing a song you know and love, but played in a different key.

I can remember the conversation that led me to loving myself. I was talking to the person I love most in the world – it's not true that you can't love someone else until you love yourself, nor that if you don't love yourself, no one else can. I told her that it didn't matter what anybody else had said, I wanted to be a father. I wanted our kids, when they materialise, to call me 'Dad'. That was really important to me. At the time, I was reading what I thought was a book about a non-binary person. I'd picked it up from the library because that's what I thought it was about, and I thought, 'Hey, great, someone like me.' It ended up not being about a non-binary person, but about a person assigned female at birth who was slowly coming to terms with the truth that they were a guy. For some reason, I'd known for 24 years that I was also a guy. It was a secret truth that I accepted, without ever verbalising, a truth that I couldn't speak, and thus could not be true unless I broke out of my solipsism. Even then, it was the woman I love who gently teased the words from me. 'Are you telling your family you're a man because you think they'll understand it better than they would you being agender? Or is it because you are a man?' she asked. I could see in her face that my truth would not diminish her love for me. 'It's because I am a man,' I replied, 'and I have to transition.'

And the funny thing is, once I'd acknowledged my true gender, I could acknowledge and embrace and love all the other bits. I could love my skin colour and my ethnicities. I could start to rid myself of internalised homophobia and misogyny, and I did. By loving myself, I have been able to love others more than I ever thought was possible. I could love, full stop.

Accepting yourself, loving yourself, frees you up to be able to live fully as the person you were meant to be. For me, he was hiding in a recess of my mind, pounding on the walls, demanding to be set free. I fobbed him off with the lie that he could only ever exist in my mind, that I had to be something different to other people. Besides, transitioning was for other people, not for me. Do you hear that? What it really meant was that happiness was for other people, not for me.

Transitioning is about living your truth. Whether it's socially, medically, spiritually – each person has their own truth and their own path. Not every path has the same waypoints, the same scenery, the same climate. And transitioning doesn't mean that things will be perfect forever and ever amen, there endeth the lesson. Sometimes (usually) it gets harder. Self-love, and the visibility that can come with walking in the world as trans, is dangerous. And sometimes it means that there is less love in your life. But the people who take their love and walk away from you don't love you, or your perception of you. They love what they think they see. They love their own perception of who you are. They might be scared that you won't need them now that you have unleashed your true self.

So in the cost-benefit analysis, why do it? For me, I couldn't go on. I saw no future as the person others were telling me I was. I got to the point where the man in the recesses of my mind eventually bashed through the walls and demanded to be taken seriously. And here we are. So now it's time to seize that love for myself.

AS EYES BLUR TOGETHER

. . . .

Ren Wilding

Once, there was a child in me
who would confess the turmoil of their mind
at midnight, their muted blue eyes
filled with guilty tears as they trembled –
a hummingbird's heart.
But there has always been this other child,
the one who sinks teeth and nails
into the blue one the moment
they think of letting go –
a cat-like desperation.
Green waits for the blue to show
a little strength, a little wildness,
a little joy to latch onto.
Green danced, their wild hair tangled and flying,
and held out their hands waiting for blue's
smile – but their mouth, a puckered rosebud,
never even giving a little twitch,
said, What is this?
My little bird, my love, will you not

come feel this? green said,
their cat eyes electrified with dancing.
But blue did not understand,
they could never be free of this constant fear.
I am not like you. I can't do this.
No, not alone, so come...hold my hands.
Blue extended their arms
and was abruptly clasped by green.
They spun together so that everything blurred
but their bodies, faces, eyes... Until they fell
and their eyes came altogether out of focus.
Blue laughed. Green cried.
And it is their stormy eyes
I now wear.

OUR BODIES DEFINE US

Freiya Benson

As I stand here naked, in front of you, I wonder what you see. I feel your eyes glancing back and forth, and I see you smile, and I think to myself, you see my body, my complicated, beautiful trans body, but what else do you see?

Do you see what I see when I look in the mirror, do you see the battles I've fought on this pale freckled landscape, or do you see something else? Do you see something more, or something less?

I have a good relationship with my body. Just reading those words though, reminds me of times when I didn't. For most of my teenage years onwards my body didn't feel like mine. I covered it up, I refused to be photographed, I hid it as much as I could. I didn't want the way I looked to be recorded, I didn't want to be reminded of what I was. I didn't want to see what I was.

My body wasn't mine, it felt wrong, and as time went by, I

started to realise why. I was trans and, worst of all, I didn't know what to do about this.

It was a stark realisation, because, honestly, there was nothing I could have done about it. When I was growing up there was no one I could talk to about it, and no information about what the way I felt meant. Sex education was strictly binary, and gender identity wasn't mentioned or even acknowledged as a thing because to most people it wasn't actually a thing anyhow.

I remember thinking that maybe I should tell someone how I felt. I even remember teachers saying that we could ask anything at all and it would be fine, but deep down I knew that if I asked about this then fine would not be part of the equation. I saw how other people who were different were bullied and attacked and ostracised, and I knew I was different. I knew the only safe thing to do was to do what I always do when I'm not sure about something.

I took what was different about me, and I buried it. I buried it deep inside, and tried to live with what I had. For a while it sort of worked, but ask anyone who's buried something and they'll all tell you the same thing – you can't bury stuff forever. The gradual erosion of living wears away whatever you cover it with, and eventually that thing gets exposed again.

No matter how much I tried to bury how I felt, it got exposed. My false body couldn't be hidden, and as I grew it rebelled against me, with unwanted hair, and height I didn't want. It pushed and shoved and demanded to be noticed. I'm not what you want, but I am what you've got. You need to love me.

And the thing is, I knew this. So I tried something else. I tried to listen, and I tried to love. How do you even begin to do that though? Where do you even start? My body was a land that had been taken from me. I wanted it back, but to do that I needed to stake a claim – but staking claims is a risky business.

You see the thing is, I'd already tried to claim back my body before. I staked my claim by starving my body.

To many people that doesn't make sense, I know, but to me it did. My body wasn't mine, so I needed to regain control over it. I did this through not eating. I could control the shape, the size, the feel of my body by deciding what I would and wouldn't put in it. I could punish my body, and I could make it listen, and then I could make it mine again.

And then that also became a way of dealing with stress, which in turn became my way of calling out for help when I couldn't manage on my own, not that I'd ever admit that I couldn't manage on my own. I'd managed on my own with this for so long that it had become a part of me, a truth hiding a lie. During these times, I know I caused myself pain, but at least I had control over my body, at least I was making a claim.

This claim, however, wasn't really a claim, it was an invasion. I remember one morning, on catching myself in the mirror and seeing my reflection, it suddenly occurred to me that this wasn't a man's body or a woman's body anymore. It wasn't any body. My invasion had conquered my body, but it had left nothing. Nothing to build on, nothing to make better, just skin and bones. This wasn't a victory, but a loss.

So I stopped, and instead tried another way. It wasn't easy – just stopping took, and honestly still takes, effort. When stressful situations happen, not eating is still my emergency response, it's just now I'm aware that it is, and that sometimes makes a difference.

I made myself rediscover my body. I spent hours looking at myself. I still do. I forced myself to look at the bits of me I hated. I looked at them and tried to think about why. I exposed myself, to myself.

I looked at my tiny boobs and reminded myself that although

they're small, they're also in proportion to the rest of me and they are beautiful.

I looked at my face, with its big nose, narrow eyes and huge mouth and I remembered how these things do make me different, but that different needn't mean bad. I remembered how as a child different meant there was something I had to hide, but as an adult, it could mean something else, something better.

I looked at my body, with its gangly limbs and awkward proportions, all scar-marked by the passing of time, and I learned to love what I saw.

I repeated these mantras, even though I didn't believe them. Over and over, time and time again, drumming them into my head so that they would create new pathways in my brain. New responses to age-old feelings of self-loathing and shame.

But it wasn't enough, not yet. So, I fell back on something I knew, something I loved. I fell back on art, and I took photographs of my body. I took naked ones and clothed ones, from above and from below. I captured parts of my limbs, and the shapes they made, and I learned to love them.

I made this a project, because if it was that then there was a purpose – because the purpose of me learning to love my body wasn't enough, not just yet. It needed another reason, something I classed as more valid, more real, more acceptable.

I took a photo of myself every day and I called it art, because this was something I knew, this was something I valued, this is something I loved.

Maybe, I think, just maybe, given time, that validity, that love will transfer onto me, and onto my body. Maybe one day, I'll take a photo, and put it on the internet, and other people will tell me how to love my body with their likes, and acknowledgement, and praise, and I'll be able to think, if all these people who don't even know me think my body is alright, then maybe I should as well.

Validity from other people isn't always a solid base to build from, but when you're building from nothing you'll take anything that's going to get those footholds, because footholds are what start you off on the climb back up to acceptance and self-worth. Who shows you where they are doesn't matter – what matters is whether you choose to use them or not.

So I kept on taking self-portraits, and I started to think to myself, I like that photograph. I started to think to myself, I look okay with some weight there, I look okay being tall, I look okay.

I staked a claim, and this time it was a claim that was recognised, a claim that worked, a claim that was valid.

And it was not just me doing this. I started noticing how other people felt the same. I noticed how my friends were all claiming their bodies back as well, using the tools they had at their disposal. I saw people marking their bodies with tattoos, staking their claim with colours and shapes and symbols of power and ownership.

I saw others standing naked and proud, allowing others to draw them, a myriad of individual interpretations surrounding them, formed in paint and charcoal, like offerings to their bodies.

Others still moved their way to ownership, twisting and turning to rhythms and beats, a ritual dance of occupancy, displayed to an enraptured crowd of onlookers.

I saw people claiming back what was taken from them, I saw people fighting long and hard to own what had been all of ours all along, even when it didn't feel that way.

And as I stand here naked, but not exposed, I remember my mantras. Words repeating, like rivers flowing in the landscape of my mind. I remember that this is a proud and strong bearing of skin and bones. I show you my body, my complicated, beautiful trans body, and I remember a time when this couldn't happen.

This piece originally appeared in Issue 237 (March 2016) of Diva.

LOVE

~~~~~~~~

Kaylie Ackerman

Sometimes when I lie down in bed, all I can feel is the ache of loneliness expanding between two cold sheets. I instinctively curl my legs up and hunch myself over, trying to remember a time when the world was small and I felt safe. Once in a while I am overtaken by a torrential flood of tears, encapsulating obscured, unprocessed feelings. Sometimes these are accompanied by choked out words such as, 'Why am I like this?' or 'Why don't you love me?' or 'Please don't leave me' or 'I don't understand'. It has been like this all my life.

When I was 5 years old I nearly drowned in the neighbours' swimming pool. Feeling invincible with a pool raft and unable to swim, I discovered that I could paddle over to the diving board in the deep end and climb aboard to cross to safety. I did this a couple of times successfully until my hands, pruned-up from splashing, lost their grip, plunging me deep into the water. I remember holding my breath as I sank down. I had been told so many times that I couldn't swim that I didn't even try. Instead, I thought maybe I could sink to the bottom and walk out to the shallow end. As my buoyancy slowed my descent I realised that I wasn't going to make it and that I was going to die. In that final moment, I thought about how my life had been short but decided that I was okay with it. I thought about my parents, who would be sad, and I hoped they would remember the best of me when they dared. And I thought about my newborn sister and wondered what she might become after I was gone. As my world grew dark, I felt sad, for all the things I would never know.

I woke up on the side of the pool with one of the neighbourhood men leaning over me. He had pulled me out and resuscitated me. After a quick checkout, he sent me home. I never told my parents what happened that summer afternoon between kindergarten and first grade, and apparently neither did he.

Carrying the secret of my near death was a strange feeling at first. But over time I became accustomed to it. So much so I rarely even connected my fear of water, or inability to complete swimming lessons, or the angst that day camp brought with its mandatory swimming activities, back to that earlier experience. I didn't dare tell my parents, afraid that the truth would erode their trust in me. Over time it kind of became an on-again, off-again secret I kept even from myself.

I am transgender, something I have always known but not always acknowledged. When I was so sure I was going to die that day, I was sad at the thought of my life ending before it really got started. But I also knew, even then, that life is painful. I'm talking about an existential pain that rises within you from a day-in and day-out lack of recognition and acknowledgement of who you are.

It's the insistence, wearing you down, that you become what everyone else needs you to be. The fear, haunting your dreams, of what other people will do if they discover your truth. The feeling, stopping you in your tracks, that nothing is right in the world. The inability, freezing your heart, to find an empathetic ear.

By the time I was a teenager I was lost, afraid and isolated in a deep depression from years of denying who I was just so I could fit in. I never fit in. For years, it was drilled into me that to be a girl when you were 'born a boy' was perverse. I could barely function in the world of men, regularly witnessing their disdain for women, expected to respond in kind, ridiculed when I did not. And I was an outcast from the world of women where no one could see me as one of their own. I was alone. I was the kid that others yelled at as they drove by, 'cut your hair, freak'. I was the skinny 'boy', wearing the pentacle charm around my neck, who men on the street would cat-call just to mock my femininity.

At age 26, I lost my virginity with a woman I had met just a week earlier. I was very attracted to her, but something didn't feel right to me. I was anxious and afraid. I had trouble staying in the moment. When I finally managed to cum I felt as if I might jump out of my skin. I ran to the bathroom, desperate to wash the shame from myself. I didn't understand any of the feelings that were rising up in me. I felt a profound disconnection within, as if something important about me had become an on-again, off-again secret that I was having trouble accessing.

Nine years earlier I sat in the office of a psychologist. He told me I was depressed and asked me point blank if I wished I was a girl. I said yes. He dangled the prospect of hormones in front of me. I went to bed that night wondering what my life could become if things worked out. I named myself Kaylie as I drifted off to sleep. I wanted this more than you can know, but in the end his terms were untenable. I would have to tell my parents and risk their acceptance and love. I would need their permission and understanding. All were in short supply, and, as with any natural resource needed to survive, the risk of absolute total loss was just too great to contemplate in that moment where I was so vulnerable, especially as it became clear that there was no guarantee of receiving help. That therapist was elated by that decision, but it has haunted me ever since.

During my thirties, the emerging world of online matchmaking became a thing. When the ache of loneliness filled every last crevice of my consciousness and I felt that I would break at any moment from my inability to even remember what it was like to be touched, I would scour free dating sites, desperate to find someone who might see me and still love me. I still remember meeting a woman and falling for her on the spot. We walked around that early fall day and made our way back to my apartment where we had sex at her urging. I can still feel how used I felt as I came to the realisation over the next few days that I was nothing but a convenient fuck for her.

Years later, I found a personal advertisement that I felt so sure about. Her idea of the perfect partner described me exactly. We agreed to meet at a funky little goth bar. She showed up a little late and apologised and then introduced me to a man she had brought with her. He was a colleague of hers and they were going out to another bar together afterwards. I sat there confused as she explained to me that she had placed the ad to try to find and help people like me. They were both 'gender therapists' and she told me that I should figure out if I was going to transition or not because, 'nothing is sadder than starting transition when you are past your prime'. Honestly, I was long ago convinced it was too late for me. I just looked on in disbelief as she patted herself on the back for doing this public service. That little stunt of hers freaked me out significantly and tainted the concept of gender therapists for me for a long time.

Instead of heeding her advice, I turned back to the internet. It was still a fresh and newish thing back then. I learned about the 'classic transsexual' and 'the autogynephile' without the slightest clue that what I was reading was utter bullshit pseudo-science. I let it freeze me in my tracks as I internalised the possibility that I was super-not-okay. I became even more isolated as my sense of self-worth was being quietly extinguished under the weight of this new information. And I concluded that I needed to stay hidden away if I wanted to be safe.

Nearly 20 years later

Three weeks after I met my wife I came out to her. The world didn't end. We married, bought a house, had a daughter; life was good by all measures. But I was still feeling lost and alone. Even though she knew I was trans, I don't think she ever expected me to transition. But after nine years together I knew I had to. Every coping strategy I had ever devised was failing me. My marriage was failing because I was so unhappy. My desire to live was failing me. And I realised that I was failing myself and everyone who was important to me by hiding my truth away.

One year later I saw a therapist I trusted, and I took hormones. Sex was no longer a sequence of mental gymnastics but was now something almost holy, present. I contemplated what the rest of my life might look like. It had been a very long time since I last allowed myself to wonder what life could be like when you are just yourself for everyone to see. To ask myself, what am I trading away and what am I gaining by embracing myself, by allowing myself to love myself? This is not in the twisted way Blanchard[14] proposes, but to truly love myself, to be kind to myself, to believe in myself. And to invite the world around me to do the same.

When I was 5, I was convinced that I couldn't swim and it nearly cost me my chance at a life. And throughout my life, people, many well-meaning, have tried to convince me that the knowledge I carry around inside – that I was born a girl – is wrong. And for a long time, I gave their words credence over my own. It's as if I have been holding my breath all these years trying to just make it to the bottom, to find release. But that is not possible. So instead I am figuring out how to swim.

Sometimes, I still climb into bed and feel the ache of loneliness in the cold sheets. And sometimes I cry uncontrollably when hidden feelings from the past resonate with my daily experience. But the words that come are not the same as before. 'What's wrong, sweetie? What is it?', my wife whispers as she holds me tight and reminds me that everything is alright, that I am not alone, that I am a good person. That I am lovable and loved.

14   Ray Blanchard, American Canadian Sexologist.

IN WEST PHILADELPHIA

Lawrence Lorraine Mullen

me saying,
i don't know what i want to do
because my body still doesn't feel right
it's been 22 years why haven't i gotten it yet

you saying,
you need to be kind to yourself

me saying,
but i need to get this right
testing out some new hormones
trying them on for size
might be rad but then
i'll be a freak

you saying,
you need to be kind to yourself
me saying,
but think about how

you'll never want to fuck me
when i look like that
i just know

you saying,
you need to be kind to yourself

me saying,
i cut my tits off
why isn't that enough
tell me why it never
seems like it will be enough

you saying,
you need to be kind to yourself
your body can only love you
if you let it.

THE BODY SUBVERSIVE

Eris Young

My body has always consisted of a disjointed collection of features. Small, slim, bony, long lashes, short hair. I am not tall. I have small hands and feet. I have an unreasonable amount of body hair. Long is the litany of complaints I've lodged against my own body since the onset of puberty, since I realised that because of it, I would never fit the conventional model of boy or girl.

Even though I don't remember ever particularly hating any one part of my body, there have been times when I've assumed myself to be undesirable, even loathsome, in the eyes of others. I knew intellectually that all people are deserving of love but at the same time felt myself undeserving of it. And there have been times when these feelings were simply a fact of life, so entrenched in my thought patterns that I had come round to them, normalised them, and taken them for granted.

I hope this is enough to convey the breathtaking clarity that comes from realising that now, today, when I plumb the depths of myself I find those same feelings simply absent. I no longer think of myself as fundamentally aberrant, separate from everyone else. Well, that's not quite right. My sexuality and my gender set me apart from most other people, but in so far as I am unique, I know it doesn't make me less than anyone else.

It's strange to look back now on who I was ten, five, even just two years ago. I've found that I think of myself as someone entirely different. Cautiously, only in the last few months, I've begun to want to know why that is. What exactly has changed to make me love, or at least accept, myself?

It's not clear when or how the change first occurred. I can think of a few events that demarcate my life now from my life then – moving to a new country, graduating, getting a full-time job and generally learning to live in the world. But the more I think about it the more I view the change as something akin to magic – an arbitrary blessing from a higher power, a boon that, no matter its origin, was in any case outside my own control. And because I felt it didn't come from inside me, it took a while to convince myself that investigation wouldn't cause my new-found self-acceptance to crumble under me and send me sliding back down the rocky slopes of depression. But I decided that whatever the cause, my new-found self-love was real. It couldn't be based on nothing, and I'd be doing myself a favour by figuring out where it came from, especially by trying to write about it.

But even after weeks of self-reflection, I haven't been able to come up with a complete answer. I know the change is connected with my mental health, which is at this point better than it's been since puberty. But I don't know which is cause, and which is effect. I've had therapy, yes, but not much, only a few intensive rounds of cognititive behavioural therapy. This therapy was focused on my symptoms – my anxiety and depression – which were in part due to dysphoria. I came out of therapy having shed thought patterns that I now know were toxic and, looking in on them from outside, completely irrational. But did therapy treat the anxiety and depression that contributed to my self-hate? Or did it treat dysphoria that, once shed, improved my anxiety and depression? The beauty of cognitive behavioural therapy is also what makes it so difficult for me to analyse; for the life of me, I can't remember a single thing my therapist actually said, but I am fully cognisant that I emerged out the other end of my sessions with a brain that felt rewired.

I think another large part of what's changed relates to control. I'm aware that for most of my life, especially at university and approaching graduation, I was plagued by a feeling of helplessness: armed with a bachelor's degree in a field I couldn't get a job in without a PhD, I felt I couldn't control my professional (and therefore my entire) future. Dysphoria played into this feeling on a more day-to-day level as I found myself unable to control how others perceived me. As long as I couldn't control how I was gendered, I couldn't interact with other (cisgender) people without a feeling of invasion, of violation. I could never feel in control of a situation.

So, perhaps predictably for a transgender person, I know that transition has been essential to the improvement in my mental health and self-acceptance. Nowadays I can control how I'm gendered by altering how I dress. In certain respects, I've even reversed the situation: sometimes when people meet me they have to ask whether I'm male or female, and when they do so I can see they are unsettled, wrong-footed by my presentation. I can straddle a proverbial line that gives me an almost giddy feeling of control.

My self-image was always intimately connected to my body image. I grew up assailed on all sides by images of airbrushed, televised, made-up men and women. I was presented with ideals, archetypes and expectations, and I knew from a very young age, as we all do, what a man and a woman should look and act like. At the same time, though, I knew for a certainty that I would never be able to achieve either ideal. Intense anxiety manifested itself when I tried to shop for clothes or go to the beach, or fill out the demographic information on a census form or a job application. I couldn't bring myself to meet anyone's eye in these situations. I didn't fit – even more, I felt myself an interloper.

For a long time, I thought this was because my body shape, my facial features and my voice meant that although I didn't consider myself a girl, I could never be taken seriously as a boy. I was barred from either category by my rejection of one and my failure – and later refusal – to cleave to the other. At the same time, though I knew that this conflict was a fact of life, as organic to me as any other aspect of my personality, it never occurred to me that it might be natural, positive or that I might have this experience in common with anyone else. This sense of aberrance and isolation is so standard for trans youth that it feels redundant to discuss it explicitly, but it had a direct and, for most of my life, unconscious effect on my sense of my own self-worth. Put simply, it made it difficult for me to see myself as a person.

When I began hormone replacement therapy I had no clear idea of what I wanted to look and sound like. With little medical oversight, it was as if I was expected to create myself. It was a second chance, as it were, to decide who I was. I dreamed vaguely of 'androgyny' without thinking practically of what this would entail in terms of vocal pitch, muscle mass and body hair. Though I realise that what I have now is what I'd wanted all along, I didn't let myself think it would be possible.

Now, in the midst of my transition, my voice is deep and warm and my upper lip has started to sprout some tentative wisps. But four years of low-dose testosterone therapy hasn't made me physically all that different from pre-transition me. I think the most pertinent change has been in my outlook – I no longer feel that lack of control over my daily life.

This feeling of control is representative of a larger kind of reversal that has defined my mid-twenties; throughout childhood and young adulthood I had dreams where disaster strikes, a family member dies, a massive change in circumstances occurs, often due to some failing of my own. The unifying feature of these dreams was not the nature of the disaster but the speed and ease with which dream-me would accept the paradigm shift and begin to adapt to it. And they were not nightmares per se. They involved circumstances which were objectively unpleasant, but the emotions attached to them were never negative; in fact, they hardly elicited any strong emotion at all from me, awake or asleep. Dream-me was adaptable: I'd be diagnosed with an incurable disease, for example, and almost before my dream-self could process the fact, I'd have begun to reconcile myself to it, to make peace, as if when disaster struck I had the power to simply choose not to be bothered.

Through this filter, I would see unpleasant aspects of my waking life not as markers of a need for a change in my or society's perspective, but as failures of my own capacity for adaptation. I thought that my dysphoria, though I didn't yet recognise it as such, was endogenous.

It came from my own inability to accept the fact of the allocation of an incorrect body in the cosmic lottery. I think I assumed, in some abstract way, that I would be happier if I could accept that I would never be happy. I didn't think far enough ahead to wonder if self-love of even the most physical sort would be a possibility once this adaptation had occurred.

Now I understand the obvious: I had misinterpreted the root of the problem. I'm not a man, nor am I a woman, and there's nothing wrong with that. I've lived in three countries and even more cultures and that has shown me a wider range of acceptable shapes and sizes of people. My discomfort with my own body, a discomfort I had tacitly accepted as permanent, has eased considerably after accepting the very obvious fact that, really, a body can take any shape and still be acceptable, valuable, desirable. And I worry less now about things I can't change. I've faced challenges and come up on top, and realised that making up stories – something I've done since before I learned to write – might be something I could do as a career. I feel a great sense of purpose in putting pen to paper. Writing allows me to interrogate myself in a way I never could before I started doing it seriously, and this in turn has allowed me to focus in a way I never could before either. Purpose and self-acceptance have helped me to feel I can occupy a place in the world, even if I don't look like most of that world's inhabitants.

There are aspects of myself, of my body, that I like now, and that I'm not ashamed for liking. My voice, chief among them, has developed nicely since I began hormone treatment. I can sing along to all my favourite brooding indie folk songs now. I like the shape of my hands if not their size, and I no longer think about how small they must appear to other people – I know other people are not so observant. My body hair still annoys me (I haven't yet worked up the nerve to visit a public swimming pool) but I categorically refuse to shave it, for political and practical reasons – getting rid of it all takes several days and several disposable razors. I don't even mind the small breasts that I once bound so painfully, and living in chilly Scotland means I no longer need to bind them, and that I can also show them off if I want to.

Most of all, though, I like the very subversion that the combination of my features – of breasts and body hair, of a deep voice and a petite frame – represents. My body is neither male nor female, it is a contradiction, and a political statement, though I never intended it to be. And I realise suddenly, even as I write this, that this was always the ideal, and at the same time as I understand this, I know that I have achieved it.

end

PALAVER

. . . .

So Mayer

I want to cast our comings, says Medusa, under
the lazy moon (or is it morning no
difference) like Emin's tissues & condoms but
shaped like between us (is nothing but grace the stereo says)
like Whiteread's hot water bottles but (obviously)
hotter, wrought of insides-
out like Hatoum's 'Corps Étranger'
exquisite says Tiresias (she's in their bed
or someone's, near the river; never the same
flat twice: they have a lot of friends
here, not [just] her) but – finger
to their lips – you'd have to keep it
wet   the clay (the lips
that have lipped hers) OK she says no kiln no
glaze   oh & a fine spray to keep them
fleshly adds T, tracing textures (like I climb
a waterfall the air sings it teases) no Medusa says
not flesh (not no to that touch yes
that is what they touch – they her imagined

sculptures; they this real person, leisurely
at her snailtongue soft garnet her they
make names for each other's apertures
apparati & extrusions so T reve[a]ls in
figurehead   lemniscate   in taper & Medusa
laughs at Boolean operator/But why? Because
it works. Because – differential-geometric of thumb & fore
finger – I found what I was searching for & so   she thinks
of her interior surfaces [at their curvature and torsion] as:
a database, search history of T [as] cursor moving inside her
as she reaches round to learn their taxonomy she
has been spending way too much time in the archive ay)
no not flesh she says but between
flesh the movements for a   curve is a topological space
locally homeomorphic will also take waveform
clay yes wet yes (yes she –) will have to keep it
liquid under her hands T adjusts their har(d)ness
(you know what you can do with those locks snakehiss
they read goldeyed as rising heat) entrance
can be read two ways a realisation as opening (that simsim
as magic   wand (waveform again   energic parabolas 3D'd by
    yearning musculature
tug-of-love gives existence to the silicon bridging (bowsprit
    googlewhack
mmmm tattoo she thinks of skin of drumskin thrumming)
T lips her, glitter eyes alive at her disappearance into thinking
but wanting (all of) her/e not as novelty
object neon keyring of her clit (now CAH is Us could use that
as a fundraiser make a note) amid that pubic turf that
rough dark doormat in whose tracery of branching gaps

their wetness jointly glints   this in
between them (in her hands thick under slip shaping it)
pocket universe into which folds third or seventh or twenty-first time
as always-first (they welcome her/e with the
tender smiles of their chest, scallop shells they sell
on a sandy seashore) first time since Athena
broke her   she is   no (fix up)   she is done
with myths of whole   this is/this is not/a given
but given all the same
given form (that heft, elastic in its weight) that in coming
to her comes apart in silver strands (when I take the angel I have a
     taste)   (pencil
she thinks I could draw   this out –   say: more
palaver their word for aftermouth mesh of talk/lick (no) clean in sight

DETRANSITION: A LOVE STORY

Evelyn Deshane

When I first met Travis, I was a boy.

This is not a poetic metaphor or a way to surprise the audience. In many love stories involving trans people, the revealing of the trans identity is done for shock value. Think of Fergus throwing up after seeing Dil's genitals in *The Crying Game*, or Brandon Teena being beaten and shot after his genitals are revealed in a similar way in *Boys Don't Cry*. When I met Travis, I had recently come out as a transgender man, but his knowledge of this was not like the movies.

It is almost never like the movies.

I transitioned precisely because the trans people on the screen were not like the trans people I met in real life. What had once seemed so far away and totally not something I identified with was suddenly something that seemed viable in person, through my trans friends. Gender could be something I could control. It was now something I wanted to play with. I could be a man, not the imitation of a man that I saw on TV.

So I instantly came out.

And I was instantly outed.

In my first week of graduate school, a well-meaning professor sent out an email to everyone about my trans status. He got it wrong, though, so I had to send out another email to correct him. Perhaps my name was too ostentatious, not to mention confusing. I'd picked Evelyn, pronounced Eve-a-lyn like the author Evelyn Waugh, and now I was regretting that choice. But it had been the first time I felt I could control what people called me, and the first time I thought I'd found a term that was wholly me and wholly mine.

This was how I met Travis – with a shaved head, newly out as trans, and going by he/him pronouns that I was adamant about people using. We bonded over the awkward email and then punk music. We became fast friends, along with two other misfit graduate students in our master's programme. There was no shock reveal of my status – at least, beyond the professor's fumbling into gender understanding. Travis would not turn to throw up or get his buddies to beat me up. He was the perfect love interest, except that we were both with other people.

Six months later, when we were both uncoupled, I had already started to question my gender yet again. I had an appointment for testosterone injection the next day. I didn't want to go. I didn't want to wear a chest-compression binder anymore, one that made it difficult to breathe and left marks up and down my body. And I didn't want to get rid of my breasts, or my uterus, or anything else. I wanted my name – I *loved* my name – but my pronouns felt more like alphabet soup most days. My adherence to gender, any gender, started to feel like another trap, something I didn't want to participate in.

But this time, there was definitely no movie I could watch, or person I could talk to in the trans community about this issue without starting a larger and more complex discussion. We don't like to talk about detransition. Because if detransition is a thing, then it pokes a hole in the common trans narrative of knowing since birth and staying the course until death. It makes doctors less likely to prescribe hormones and surgeons hesitate to operate. Detransition makes the trans movement and community go backwards. It gives conservative pundits a reason to kick trans women out of bathrooms. Detransition is a dirty word. It is a violent word.

And after coming out so publicly, I couldn't exactly go back into the closet, nor did I want to either. But to stay on the path I had chosen still made me feel odd. Detransition seemed like my only option, but I couldn't find support.

Except for Travis.

He was the only person I talked to during this time period about my gender and its complications. He didn't tell me to stop. He didn't tell me to continue. But he listened. He raised interesting questions. He emailed me late one night, and told me that he liked to call me Eve, a shortened version of my full name, because, like Eve in the Bible, she was still made from Adam – the first man – but she was also different. She was the first woman before gender politics.

That was the moment I knew I was in love with him. Adam and Eve, together, lost in paradise and falling in love. I knew I wanted to be with Travis in that moment.

A week later, we kissed in his apartment's front hallway.

I cancelled the testosterone appointment I had been postponing.

My gender fell away.

Detransition became a love story.

For a long time, I thought a detransition narrative needed to be one where I stripped down everything that I had done before. I stopped the doctor's appointments, I gave away my binders, I bought women's clothing again, and I grew out my hair. After a year together, Travis and I both moved to a new town where no one knew my previous history. He called me his partner, a nice gender-effacing term, and we went on with our lives. I wasn't exactly cis, but I couldn't be trans anymore, right? I had no doctor involvement. I had no links to the community anymore, since I'd left them in a previous town. And because detransition was still a slippery slope and a dirty word, I had no story to tell. My history was gone. I tried to start again as something new, but there was still something nagging and incomplete. I couldn't tell people how I'd met Travis, not completely, because it would mean blotting out what was so significant. When we fell in love, I was a boy. Then I wasn't a boy.

Now I'm something else entirely, but mostly, I'm Eve.

And I became Eve when I was with him.

When that email came around the school and outed me, I'd already accepted the fact that identity was contextual. If people didn't know about my trans identity, I could never be addressed how I wanted to be. So I had to come out, and come out, and come out. But I never truly considered that gender itself was contextual at its core. There was no true self inside me begging to get out, but a situation that I wanted to feel over and over again. I thought it meant I had to be a man, because being a girl and woman had been so difficult in my past. But being a man, whatever that meant, wasn't exactly what I was looking for either. The feeling I craved was recognition, and I got that when I was Eve.

And being Eve meant being together, alone in paradise, with someone who understood.

Gender was a love story, one that could not be complete without Travis. One that could not ever be complete without someone else. And so detransition didn't have to be a dirty word or the complete eradication of everything that had come before. Detransition was my happy ending.

Detransition was moving in together. A proposal. And now, soon to be a wedding. While planning our wedding, I made the joke that its theme would be 'no god no gender'. But I know that's not quite true. The gender is always there. Nothing is ever gone or left behind. It's a soft gender, like the soft kind of love that visits me every morning, whispering 'Eve' into my ear, but it's enough to make me believe in paradise all over again.

♡

ON LOVE – THE PAST AND FUTURE OF LOVE

~~~~~

**What advice would you give your past
self when it comes to love?**
....

She's waiting for you, no matter what stage of life she finds you in.

Dare loving. The pain of unrequited love proves your heart is still beating.

You are okay, no matter who you are, which gender you have and how you feel. It is okay to love.

Don't stay with someone because you don't want to be alone. Longing for company isn't love.

I'd advise them to read bell hooks's book *All About Love* which explains how love isn't possible in situations of injustice – you have to value yourself and the other person, or people, equally. It won't work if you value them way more than you, or vice versa.

Just as I suspected, you don't owe anyone your love.

Put yourself out there. Go to trans groups where people meet for friendships and more. Just don't be afraid. Don't think so much about your so called 'baggage'. Imagine just how easily and how much you could love someone in the exact same situation as you. Be unapologetic.

You don't need to try to help those partners of yours as much as you did. Whether they meant to or not, they took from you and it was never really a fair transaction. It's so trite, but only because it is so goddamn true, that you must above all else learn how to love yourself. You are all you have in this world and everything stems from you. You deserve to love yourself, you are worthy of loving yourself and you are capable of loving yourself. Once you learn how to do this, you can go to places which you never dreamed could even exist.

Love yourself first, as lame as that sounds. Don't lose yourself in someone else – you are more than just one half of a relationship.

Be patient. Be prepared. Be open.

You will never feel loved by your family. You will debase yourself and humiliate yourself, you will fight and scream and cry, you will plead and cajole, you will hide and deny and you will never get them to love you the way you want them to. And that's actually okay.

Don't bother.

Don't give up.

Love with all your heart.

Let it happen.

There is a very real difference between loving someone and being in love with them.

Avoid love, lust and a taste for the finer things in life – they will not bring lasting happiness and will only impede you.

Make sure you love each other for the right reasons. Be honest as early as possible. Don't fuck it up.

Let love come to you. Don't chase it desperately as you'll encounter all the wrong people. You are worthy of a deep, unconditional love. You are worthy of people who will treat you well. Toxic people will come and go, and fail to break your spirit.

Measure and take stock of everything else you are loading the word 'love' with.

Friendships are as important as romantic/erotic relationships – in fact, they're what you're trying to get to. It's a total cliché, but in my case it's proven true. I'm still friends with many ex-lovers (not all, not the mean ones. That's important too – don't love people who hurt you, condescend to you, abuse you – your love cannot change them, it can only fuel them) and ex-crushes. Give your time to nurture friendships, however you can, even if that means online. And be prepared to be surprised that you can love your family, on the other side of remaking yourself (again, it's not true for everyone, and I do not love all members of my biological family, but it's piercing how much love I can feel for some of them). Also, it's not impossible or impractical to love yourself. Don't share Audre Lorde's ideas and believe they don't apply to you – you will be utterly astonished, overwhelmed and regenerated by what can happen if you give yourself permission to love yourself. (But don't blame yourself for taking the time to learn how to do this.)

Don't love someone just because you like the idea of being in a relationship, or because it's become a habit to love them. Only love them if they make you happy.

I would tell myself that even love would not help me to run away from the reality of who I was and what I am. I would tell myself that if I follow my heart and fall in love my true self will not be suppressed and, like a poisoned arrow, I will destroy everyone I love, including my soulmate.

Love without conditions. Ask nothing more from love than you are willing to give. Never define how someone should love you. Just be glad they do.

Relax and let the world happen to you for a bit.

What hopes and dreams do you have for the future, in relation to love?

I would love to have a partner. I would love for them to maybe be trans too so they understand me in every way. I would love to have our own place to live – no matter how crappy and tiny, it would be ours. I would love to be married and have pets.

I would like to meet someone and fall in love. I would love that. I enjoy being on my own but there's a part of me which really wakes up and thrives on having a partner or partners. In the short term, I want to travel and meet people. In the long term, who knows? I hope that my life will always be filled with love.

I'd find some hunk that loves me and all the messy shit that comes along with that.

Marriage, children...a family. A normal sense of life with consistency, kindness and togetherness.

I want me and my wife to live forever. I want us to be that unfriendly couple in the scary house at the end of the street that is slightly dilapidated, with the curtains always closed, that the neighbourhood children dare each other to ring the doorbell of. And when we answer we'll always be grumpy and one of us will shout something like, 'Those pesky kids' and the other will say, 'Leave them alone, they're just children having fun. We used to do that when we were young,' but at Halloween we'd be famous for having the scariest decorations but also the best sweets and people would know that we are actually kind and wonderful, and that we are the greatest love story ever told.

None.

I'm heartbroken, I can't see myself loving again.

More of the same.

I hope love finds me because I've given up looking!

To never feel so incomplete that I succumb to the desire to belong to another.

Not that many. Just need to learn to appreciate someone and trust in them.

To maintain happy and stable relationships. To know my worth and not settle for less.

I want to keep choosing my lover for a lifetime.

adrienne maree brown talks in her book *Emergent Strategy* about 'coevolution through friendship' as the core of progressive movements. I really like this idea. I'd like to see love talked about more outside its narrow cishet-norm confines, and taken away from fantasies of domination, ownership and whiteness. I want to be open to messiness rather than perfection in love/s, and to think more about what it means to have familial, friendly, romantic, erotic and other kinds of love to take place in the same spaces. I want to think about getting rid of the melodrama around love, and seeing it as practical – as intentional labour, a practice of loving rather than a fixed notion of love.

I want to be with the person I love now forever. I want us to stay as in love as we always have been.

I'm engaged to be married and I'm looking forward to a happy life with my spouse.

I would like to find a boyfriend. If love develops, then so be it.

More...I'm terribly greedy. It would be nice to fall in love with someone from the same city.

PART 6

LOVE, AND ALL OF US

Over the year it's taken me to make this book, I've thought a lot about love. It's made me think about how I experience love, and how much that's changed over the years. I've come from a place where I thought love was completely unobtainable for me, because of being trans. I saw this part of me as a barrier to love, whether that was in relation to others or myself.

Love, for me, was, and sometimes still is, hard to do, and I know I'm not alone in feeling this. I've been told so many amazing positive things from other trans people about their relationships with love, but I've also heard from people who haven't had things go so well for them. I've heard from people whose marriages have collapsed because they came out, who have lost everything they hold dear, who've experienced love as a destructive and cruel thing that only hurts.

And I get that. For a long time, I saw love as something other people had, and something that I wasn't allowed.

But then I found love. Not just once either. Yes, it was hard, yes, being trans did impact a lot on how things went, but it still happened. I discovered that old friends still loved me and that new friends were out there just waiting to be met. I had relationships with people, and I dated, and it was (mostly) okay.

I had to push myself, and I had to challenge myself, and yeah, there were tears. I saw a counsellor and I learned how to love myself more. I shared how I was feeling with people I trust. I tried my very best to stay alive and to believe in hope, because even when times got dark I needed to believe that it would get better.

I put so much effort into love, because otherwise all I'd have left would be hate, and I'd experienced enough hate. Because ultimately that's what it's all about. It's about challenging the dark, the hate, the negative. It's about us being good people. It's about love.

Anyone can be an asshole, it's easy. Hell, sometimes it's too easy. Being a good person, a kind person, a person who loves, that takes effort.

I could hate. I've got plenty of reasons to. I could hate the person who shouted cruel and derogatory words at me in the street last week; I could hate the trolls on Twitter who attack the charity I work for because we work with trans young people; I could hate the people who say I'm not a real woman and reduce my identity to what bits they perceive me to have, rather than what I know in my heart and mind; I could hate the people who say I don't deserve a voice, who deny my existence, erase my identity and try to crush my soul.

Oh I could hate and it would be endless and all-consuming.

I could wear my pain and fury like a coat of flames and everyone would know and everyone would see.

Except...

That coat, that fire isn't going to save me, it's only ever going to consume me. I'd just be another angry voice in a sea of angry voices. And that's not good enough anymore. I need to take that anger and fire and make it a part of me. I need to let it fuel me, not burn me. My anger, our anger, is one of the most powerful tools we have for change, because it's so relentless and so full on. It is easy to forget that sometimes.

And actually, I don't just mean our anger, our fire and our passion as trans people either. I mean all of us. Trans, cis and everything in between.

Just imagine how strong we would all be together, how much we could all change, if we just stopped fucking shouting at each other. Just imagine what we could do if we recognised our similarities rather than our differences.

Putting this book together, and hearing from the remarkable people who have contributed has been an honour, and I feel privileged that so many people wanted to share their experiences, feelings and stories. There's so much here that I've learned from, so much that I've felt solidarity with.

This is so important as well. Listening to someone else and their experiences is a powerful thing. It can give us understanding, a new perspective and insight we didn't have before. It can give us humanity and empathy. When we don't have these things, we stop caring, we become cold and empty and our world grows small. We stop listening, we stop learning and we get stuck in hate, fear and prejudice.

And in this small world, without humanity, with empathy, it's suddenly okay to be cruel. It's okay to say whatever you want on the internet, even if it's transphobic or racist or misogynistic. It's normal to voice hateful opinions, shallowly disguised as 'debates', to shout abuse in the street at people who are different from you, to write newspaper articles filled with vitriol and hostility towards trans people, or refugees, or whoever finds themselves the latest target for hate. In this small world, it's standard to push people so far over the edge that they kill themselves, and then laugh it off and call them snowflakes because they dared to feel. It's fine if the people in positions of power exploit and hurt other people. It's okay if they say that actually you can't have the choice to decide what bathroom to use, or if you want an abortion or not, or even if it's okay to live in this country. In a small world, it's everyone for themselves, fuck empathy, screw caring, long live hate.

When we live in a small world we lose our ability to love, and when we lose that then the small world just becomes the world. I don't know about you but I don't want to live in that world. I don't want to live in a world where being a kind, caring human being is seen as a weakness, as a flaw, as something to be mocked and exploited. Honestly, why would any of us want to live in that world?

And yet here we are.

So now, more than ever, we need a new mantra. A mantra based on love, not hate. We need to come together, we need to do better, and we need to start loving. We need to hear about other people's struggles, triumphs, loves and losses. We need to listen, and also we need to talk. We need to talk about our shared experiences and our differences because then we start to empathise and care for each other. And that, my beautiful, amazing friends, will bring us closer together, it will make us kinder and it will make us better.

So be kind. Be good. Love with all your heart.

If you only learn to love one thing, make it yourself. If all of you is too much at first, then start with something small. Find the one bit of you that you do love and work from there. Nurture it, care for it and let it grow.

Remember that you are amazing. Remember that you deserve love. Remember that being trans should never be a limiter on that.

Love is a fundamental human right. No exceptions, no excuses, no buts.

Speak out against hate and intolerance when you can, and encourage your friends, your families, your people, to speak up when you can't. We're all in this together, all 7.6 billion of us. Know that this isn't a debate.

Know that being trans, being worthy of love, being free to express your true trans self, never was a debate. We are, and always will be, real.

You are never entirely alone, even when it feels as if you're in the darkest place in the universe.

Hear that I found love, despite what I thought, and know that I believe you can too.

Remember there are other people like you, even when you feel certain that there aren't. We've got each other. We've got you.

Don't be afraid to be who you are, even if the cost seems unbearably high.

It's not just you.

When you start to love yourself, the rest will follow.

You are amazing, and you deserve love.

AUTHOR BIOGRAPHIES

Alex Ahmed is a trans woman of Turkish and Pakistani ancestry currently living in Boston, Massachusetts. She is a graduate student and union organiser at Northeastern University, and can be found on Twitter and Wordpress as @WomensFormula.

Meg-John Barker is the author of a number of popular books on sex, gender, and relationships, including *Queer: A Graphic History, How to Understand Your Gender, Enjoy Sex (How, When, and IF You Want To), Rewriting the Rules, The Psychology of Sex* and *The Secrets of Enduring Love*. They have also written a number of books for scholars and counsellors on these topics, drawing on their own research and therapeutic practice. www.rewriting-the-rules.com, www.megjohnandjustin.com. Twitter: @megjohnbarker.

Freiya Benson is a 40-something trans woman who lives by the sea. She mostly writes about love, relationships and being trans, and her work has been published in *Ladybeard, i-D,* the *Huffington Post* and *Diva* magazine, which also once ran a full-page photo of her holding one of the chickens that lives in her garden. She also takes photographs, and her pictures have appeared in *NME* and *Diva*, among others. This is her first time editing an anthology. www.freiyabenson.com.

Sebastian Causton is a nerdy, usually confused person who writes about the trials and tribulations of queer life. Seb started performing poetry in 2017 and through a bunch of good luck has performed at Hammer & Tongue, Trope, Devil's Dyke Network, The Peripheral Visionaries Festival, The Royal Albert Hall and supported Lemn Sissay. This is Seb's first publication. Twitter and Facebook: @SCaustonPoetry.

Sabah Choudrey is a hairy brown transgender Muslim who likes talking and writing and feelings. Sabah co-founded Trans Pride Brighton in 2013 and has worked with queer, trans and non-binary youth since 2014. Psychotherapist in training. Social justice fighter in training. Top three passions right now: carving out spaces for queer and trans desi community, making friends with cats and taking selfies from bad angles. sabahchoudrey.com. Facebook: Sabah Choudrey. Twitter: @SabahChoudrey. Instagram: @sabah.c.

Sid S. Coles is a career free-ranger who answers to the call for hard work in the social justice and humanitarian domains. Writing is a preferred medium of engagement around love, equality, compassion and truth-seeking. Currently doing a second PhD, Sid wants everyone to know it really is never too late to learn new tricks.

Faith DaBrooke is a transgender woman and author who lives in Brooklyn. Her weekly podcast *The Gender Rebels* has an average of over 1400 downloads per episode and her weekly blog *Adventures* *of a Gender Rebel* receives an average of over 600 daily views. She is also known to many through her former YouTube channel *GenderFlux Revolutionary*, which was one of the first transgender themed YouTube channels.

Evelyn Deshane's creative and non-fiction work has appeared in *Plenitude Magazine*, *Briarpatch Magazine*, *Strange Horizons*, *Lackington's* and *Bitch Magazine*, among other publications. Evelyn (pron. Eve-a-lyn) received an MA from Trent University and is currently completing a PhD at the University of Waterloo. Evelyn's most recent project, *#Trans*, is an edited collection about transgender and non-binary identity online. Visit evedeshane. wordpress.com for more information.

Ariel Estrella (they/them), who hails from Queens, New York City, is a queer Latinx scholar who focuses their advocacy on fostering beloved communities. For three years, they headed a column for their college newspaper on the politics of love. They will soon be pursuing doctoral research on queer of color lyricism. Their writings have been included in anthologies published by Arsenal Pulp and Tia Chucha Press. www.arielestrella.com.

Peta Evans is a queer, non-binary gendered artist and writer, and an ordained minister in the Metropolitan Community Church. Their partner is also non-binary and an artist, and their lives focus around creating beautiful things, supporting their communities, gardening, and being ridiculously devoted to their pet dog, Marmite.

Jo Green describes themself as a non-binary person who's a part-time wordsmith. As well as contributing to this anthology, they've authored two books, *Queer Paganism* and *The Trans Partner Handbook: A Guide for When your Partner Transitions*, as well as being the lyricist of the queer punk band Pentacorn. They run Distinction Trans & Partner Support as well as having a full-time corporate job (entirely unrelated to anything else they do).

Max Guttman (ze/zir/zirs) is a non-binary transgender and Ashkephardi Jewish educator, artist and writer. Ze is passionate about making education accessible, liberating and fun. Originally from Rockville, Maryland, Max currently lives in Boston where ze works for a certain fruit-based technology company. www.maxguttman.com.

mud howard is a non-binary trans poet from the states. mud is co-editor of the blackout queer zine project pnk prl. they write about queer intimacy, interior worlds and the cosmic joke of the gender binary. their work has been published in *THEM* journal, *The Lifted Brow* and *Cleaver Magazine*, from which their poem was selected for The Best of the Net 2017. www.mudhoward.com.

Alex Iantaffi (they/them or he/him) PhD, MS, LMFT, SEP, CST is a therapist, Somatic Experiencing® practitioner, writer and independent scholar. They are a trans masculine, non-binary, bi queer, disabled, Italian immigrant witch who has been living, loving and parenting on Dakota and Anishinaabe territories, currently known as Minneapolis (US), since 2008. Alex co-authored *How to Understand Your Gender* with Meg-John Barker (Jessica Kingsley Publishers) and is the host of the *Gender Stories* podcast. www.alexiantaffi.com. Twitter: @xtaffi.

Aglaya Khachaturian. Nothing to see here.

So Mayer (she/they) is a writer and activist. Recent books include *Political Animals: The New Feminist Cinema, From Rape to Resistance: Taking Back the Screen* (available at PayPal.me/troublemayer/5), and the poetry collections *(O)* and *kaolin, Or How Does a Girl Like You Get to Be a Girl Like You?*; and a chapbook, *<jacked a kaddish>*. So works with queer feminist film curators Club des Femmes and campaign/community Raising Films. Current project: www.tinyletter.com/sophiemayer. Twitter: @troublemayer

Lawrence Lorraine Mullen (they/them) is a non-binary Philadelphia-based poet and graduate student pursing an MFA in Poetry at Arcadia University. They have been published in *Crab Fat*, *Pomona Valley Review*, *GTK Creative*, *Ghost City Review* and *Spiral Poetry I*.

Caleb Murray is a 27-year-old non-binary transmasculine person, living in the south-west of Scotland. Much of their work is poetry, which covers personal experiences as well as thought-provoking pieces surrounding queer and disability activism. One of Caleb's favourite pastimes is playing with their family westie called Scott. https://calebswritingspace.wordpress.com.

Grace E. Reynolds is a writer, coder, photographer and filmmaker in southern Oregon. Her work deals with the politics of identity, the friction of rubbing against societal expectations, and the resulting fall-out. She's been published in *Toyon* and *The Steelhead Review*, and she co-founded the Redwood Coast Writers' Center.

Roch is thoroughly enjoying his second puberty, and the feeling that his body is starting to resemble more of a home. He enjoys running, lifting heavy things, cabbage and fizzy sweets. Find him on Instagram: @necasterine (non-running) and @runningonbiscuits (running).

Ryan is a youth worker, an avid reader and a countryside lover. He lives with his partner and many, many books. He makes 'dad jokes' way too often, thinks he is much funnier than he actually is and spends far too much time on his PlayStation.

Kaoru Sato is a genderqueer musician, photographer and writer from London. Currently active in the bands Deathline, Weird Sex and Easterhead, they originally gained notoriety with transgender punks Six Inch Killaz. Sato's photographic work can be seen at The Dead Zoo: http://thedeadzoo.com. Their now defunct weblog, the draGnet, was named among one of the '100 best British blogs' by *.net Magazine*. *The Bends* is their first published work of fiction.

Deeana Violet is in her forties and dresses like a beatnik. She teaches film to teenagers for a living, all of whom are used to the savage heels and gothy eyeliner by now. For fun, she writes spooky little stories on strange photos and then puts them on the internet. She needs to get out more.

Ren Wilding is a queer, non-binary trans word activist and parrot caregiver. They work to share their experience as a person with mental illness to render neurodivergence as familiar. They have graduate degrees in literature and gender studies and have previously been published in *The Outrider Review* and *Cactus Heart*.

Eris Young is a queer writer who moved from Southern California to Edinburgh for the lit scene and, apparently, the damp. They write speculative fiction and essays that interrogate queer themes, and their work has appeared in *Bewildering Stories, Esoterica, Scrutiny Journal* and, most recently, Knight Errant Press's anthology, *F, M or Other: Quarrels with the Gender Binary*. They can be found tweeting at @young_e_h.

FURTHER RESOURCES AND READING

Allsorts Youth Project – Brighton-based LGBTU (lesbian, gay, bi, trans or unsure/exploring) youth project. allsortsyouth.org.uk.

Gendered Intelligence – Trans and gender variant youth organisation, based in London. genderedintelligence.co.uk.

Genderfork – A supportive community for the expression of identities across the gender spectrum. www.genderfork.com.

Mermaids – UK charity that supports children and young people who are trans and/or gender diverse, and their families. www.mermaidsuk.org.uk.

National Centre for Transgender Equality – A non-profit organisation working to improve rights for trans people in the USA. www.transequality.org.

Stonewall – UK based LGBT rights charity. www.stonewall.org.uk.

Trans Lifeline – Trans-led national helpline in the USA and Canada. www.translifeline.org.

Before I Step Outside. (You Love Me) by Travis Alabanza, travisalabanza.co.uk.

Gender Failure by Rae Spoon and Ivan E. Coyote, Arsenal Pulp Press.

Improvise, Girl, Improvise by Lilith Latini, Topside Press.

Lighter Than My Shadow by Katie Green, Jonathan Cape.

Nameless Woman: An Anthology of Fiction by Trans Women of Color by Venus Selenite, Ellyn Pena and Jamie Berrout, www.transwomenwriters.org.

Nevada by Imogen Binnie, Topside Press.

Outside the XY: Black and Brown Queer Masculinity edited by Morgan Mann Willis, Riverdale Avenue Books.

Queer: A Graphic History by Meg-John Barker and Julia Scheele, Icon Books.

Queer Sex by Juno Roche, Jessica Kingsley Publishers.

Small Beauty by Jia Qing Wilson-Yang, Metonymy Press.

The Gender Games by Juno Dawson, Two Roads.

The New Girl: A Trans Girl Tells It Like It Is by Rhyannon Styles, Headline.

The Trans Partner Handbook by Jo Green, Jessica Kingsley Publishers.

This Modern Love by Will Darbyshire, Arrow Books.

To My Trans Sisters by Charlie Craggs, Jessica Kingsley Publishers.

#Trans: an anthology about transgender and nonbinary identity online edited by Evelyn Deshane.

Which One is the Bridge by Charles Theonia, Topside Press.

Your Silence Will Not Protect You by Audre Lorde, Silver Press.